In Search of a
Stress-Free Life

Alfred L. Anduze, MD

YorkshirePublishing
www.yorkshirepublishing.com
Write Now.

Yorkshire Publishing
3207 South Norwood Avenue
Tulsa, Oklahoma 74135
www.YorkshirePublishing.com
918.394.2665

CONTENTS

DEDICATION

This book is dedicated to all the people who like myself have had a difficult time in the recognition and management of stress.

ACKNOWLEDGEMENTS

Thank you to all those humans without enough to eat, or a decent shelter or clothes to wear, who endure insults daily of being told they are not good enough because they reside in a certain place or the color of their skin is not acceptable you are the classic results of pure stress, both environmental and emotional.

To those doctors who question the risk factors of diseases and the healing capacity of their patients without looking at the contribution of the stress they are experiencing. Perhaps a little consideration of how stress determines responses can lead to better outcomes.

To the people of Ikaria, Greece, who are striking examples of how low stress levels contribute to longevity, happiness and high quality of life.

To Professor Edward Rowe, literary scholar of Ireland and Switzerland, first of all, for reconnecting and secondly, for pointing out the management of stress throughout classical and modern literature, some effective and some, dramatically immersed in tragedy.

To my wife, Sariluz, for her diligent first readings, her detection skills and attention to details are legendary.

And to my editor, Liselie Soto, for a thorough job, as always.

Other medical books by Alfred L. Anduze, MD

Pterygium: A Practical Guide to Management (2009)
An Integrative Medicine Approach to Modern Eye Care (2014)
Natural Health and Disease Prevention (2016)
First Aid on the Farm (2017)
Primeros auxilios en la granja (2017)

PREFACE

There are many journal articles and well researched volumes written about how to deal with stress. I have read extensively about management strategies, coping and overcoming established stressors but came away dissatisfied and unclear as to what exactly to do. How does it work? How do I "get rid of the bad feeling"? Despite whatever techniques or strategies used, a short while later, the stressor is still there and my response immediately or eventually reappeared. I could only ignore an unpaid bill for so long. I could only pretend that a rival is not stabbing me in the back on a daily basis. I could only tolerate the person who was harassing me openly or behind my back ... but for so long. I could only work toward an end and watch it tumble down as result of outside pressure or inside ineptitude, for a few times. Stress is pervasive. It affects everyone, albeit to different degrees, and the effect is to cope, or be overwhelmed. Ignoring it leads to the eventuality of succumbing, exploding or imploding.

So what makes this book different from all the others about stress? After receiving a firm recognition that stress is a real biochemical and physiological entity; an identification of the various causes; an examination of the multiple linkages and associations with disease; and a listing of the various modes and strategies that could be used to mitigate the response, an organized mode of stress control is provided in chapter five. This "Stress-free Life Plan" is a template designed to suit the individual. You identify your stressors, stress levels and choose your options to fit the situation.

Understanding the mechanisms of stress is essential to finding adequate relief. Hence the first chapter deals with how stress is generated, magnified and persists in our daily lives. Biochemically, the release of stress hormones, cortisol and adrenalin, lead to the stress response. The reactions can be acute, which is healthy and necessary for survival, or chronic, which most often leads to compromise of the organism and eventually debilitating diseases. Though we are genetically and environmentally wired for stress hormone release and reaction, our reptile-mammalian brains are still somewhere between the Stone Age and Medieval times. Modern stressors overwhelm our biological capacities. Stress hormone release is now constant and our physiological chemistry is often in a chronic state of full reaction.

Having been in medical practice for over 40 years, a vast majority of the patients I have seen were suffering from high levels of "total body inflammation" which was directly associated with their disease processes. For example, a 60 year old individual with diabetes, hypertension, arthritis, and early cancer, will more than likely also have a history of chronic recurrent stress. *Repeatedly high stress hormone release is linked to disease processes.* On many occasions, lectures, presentations, I have advocated the inclusion of C- reactive protein (CRP) levels in all patients as part of routine blood work in order to identify abnormal inflammation levels in the body. In addition to treating the disease, one should address and reduce the inflammation as well as remove the cause of the disease. When only the disease is treated, the cause may still persist. This is the way that Stress works. Unless the cause is addressed or the response changed or removed, the result will still be the same.

To deal with stress and response, inflammation and disease, I approached stress management along the lines of six basic strategies of healthy living. Exercise, Nutrition, Social Connections, Mental Stimulation, Avoidance of Risky Behavior and Stress Control, as described in *Natural Health and Disease Prevention*, become an integral part of the whole patient health care.

As a product of the 1960's, I made my achievements and accomplishments on my own (i.e. before affirmative action), weathered the pitfalls and schemes designed to hold back people of color, foreigners, and whatever the hell I was at that time. I approached the stress I encountered in a haphazard way, not knowing what it was and certainly not in possession of any methods with which to handle it. Inadvertently, I made it through using the six basic strategies of healthy living as presented by Andrew Weil, MD, in his Integrative Medicine Course for physicians at the University of Arizona. I did weekly exercise (sports); ate a healthy balanced diet (had gained over 25 pounds during medical school and then reduced on my own to a comfortable Body Mass Index of 21.9, where I remain fifty years later); studied, read and continued to learn new things (mental stimulation); tried to keep friends and family close (social connections); and avoided bad habits (smoking, drugs legal and illegal, though I like my glass of wine with dinner) and exposure to toxins. I did all of those strategies successfully, BUT still struggled daily and mightily with Stress Management.

Amidst the successes and achievements of 40 years of patient care, chronic Stress and frustration were interwoven and expressed almost on a daily basis. The demands of technology, surgeries, medications, acquisitions, property, material, reputation, plus the fact that the successes were envied by others led to difficulties that were most often man-made. Overworked and harboring a deep fear of bureaucrats, colleagues and patients, my stress levels were off the charts. On the verge of total "burnout", I had to learn to deal effectively with my own stress levels. Though there were many relaxation techniques and coping strategies, once (in effect), the stressors were still there.

In addition, my own tendencies to bite off more than I can chew, property issues, coupled with family matters and basic daily racist attitudes, I realized early on that a completely "stress-free life" may be unattainable. Simple things like one's successes, people who know better are intent on pulling you down. Your own excesses are often wide open target to failure...properties, materials, prestige, level of existence. When you think all is well, another crisis appears...usually linked to people and personalities. When at full throttle, we are bombarded with stressors on a daily basis and how we handle the response determines what quality of life we will lead. My patients with glaucoma, diabetes, hypertension, arthritis, cancer... all were treated with the most modern techniques and care that often "stressed" their bodies and minds and bank accounts out beyond repair.

Though Stress may have been mentioned briefly as a contributing factor in most western medical practices, most often it is brushed off as we rush to reduce symptoms armamentarium of drugs and surgical techniques. Very seldom does one bother to find the root cause of anything. What is most striking is that we are looking at the causes directly. We should be able to see the direct association of disease with stress related hormonal activity associated with metabolic dysfunction. My suggestion to physicians is to question your patients directly and extensively.

Almost every case of cancer, arthritis, hypertension, heart disease, gastrointestinal dysfunction, urinary tract malfunction, and even progressive glaucoma is associated one way or another with chronic stress factors leading to inflammation, compromised circulation, abnormal blood and fluids chemistry, and ultimate cellular, tissue and organ damage.

Since cause, effect, and disease associations are normal occurrences in life, we aim to influence the various responses. Though there are generally four strategies of stress response, acceptance, adaptation, alteration and avoidance, we lean toward the latter two as being the most effective. Finally, the ultimate suggestion for stress control is the creation of your own personal stress-free life plan where it may be easier and more practical to pursue and achieve an organized life with a minimum of stress.

By virtue of our human condition and the characteristics of the planet we live on, by where and how we lived and by the character of our fellow inhabitants, and the fact that even with coping devices in play, many stressors remain. Though I retired on time and with a good plan, many stressors, some of the same, some new, and some totally unexpected were still present. The Garden of Eden, Paradise, Nirvana, probably will not be attained in this human life, but given the right circumstances and substantial effort, we could come close. In stress management, the stressor should be identified; the response modified to elicit minimum inflammation, the disease should be treated for the organism to return to the optimum state of homeostasis.

With elaborate ways to achieve Stress Relief such as coping techniques, brain manipulation, meditation, biological feedback, all of which are good, the next day or next minute, the stressor is still there. It was simply ignored for a while. Why not AVOID the stressor all together? Stress management can be more effective if aimed at removal of the stressor, either directly or indirectly or transformation of the response from chronic to acute or by development of a strong immune system which can defend against the disease process associated with stress.

Taking steps toward avoidance of the stressor and its effects can be a very rewarding strategy.

I wrote this book so that I could learn better ways to manage stress and hopefully impart it to others. Not that there is a perfect solution to all stress, but if a few practical strategies can help to reduce the stress response by 1 inch or 1 ounce then it will be well worth the effort. When you finish this book, you should be able to outline and follow the basic steps needed to set up your own "stress-free life plan" using the tools and suggestions in chapter four, Stress Management.

Alfred L. Anduze, MD

INTRODUCTION

*"Stress is when you wake up screaming and re-
alize you haven't fallen asleep yet."*
YOURS TRULY (BUMPER STICKER)

*"Every human encounters stress, both in phys-
ical and emotional form. It is our response to
stress that determines the success or failure of
its management."*
HANS SELYE

In **Search of a Stress-free Life** is not only a book about stress
and the factors that keep us on edge, but is a practical guide
that attempts to provide realistic suggestions on the nature and
management of stress, condensed into the form of a simple template by which the individual can tailor the stress response and
achieve definitive relief.

The purpose of the book is twofold: first, it outlines and ex-
plains the realities of Stress and the Stress response, and second,
it provides a template of options for the possible resolution of
stress-related issues for the average person, as opposed to suggestions and remedies that require close psychological supervi-
sion. The following are some basic facts concerning stress:

From the inception of man as *Homo sapiens*, the first thought
has been on longevity. "How do I survive" developed into "how
do I live longer and better?" and then became, "How do I live
without stress".

Stress occurs in both acute and chronic forms, and in both physical and emotional forms. It is a direct cause of Inflammation, which is highly associated with Disease. So many of our communities are physically toxic and emotionally based on fear they only foster jealousy, anger, resentment, and anxiety. Both are intricately associated with unhealthy conditions. Stress rivals an inadequate diet and lack of physical activity as a major cause of poor health.

The first and most important requirement for successful stress management is GOOD HEALTH.

For a successful encounter with stress, one needs to understand the mechanisms of Cortisol release, the feelings associated with it and how to reduce its presence. Though the reactions may differ, the biochemistry of Stress is the chemistry of cortisol. Some people thrive on acute stress. It provides them with motivation. A more frequent and intense event may lead to a more gratifying response. It may be the essence of their existence. For some people, crisis management is their lifeblood. The need to have an adversary, or someone or something to hate and fear is their reason for being. On the other hand, for most human beings, the exposure to chronic stress more often leads to disability and disease.

Vignette #1: *The following is my most recent personal experience with Hurricane Maria, while alone on my mountain farm. Believing myself to be ready to face winds around 180 mph, my 69 year old male blood pressure started out at 140/95 (It is normally 125/80). About an hour into the storm, with rain penetrating windows like they weren't there, my blood pressure went up to 145/100, and I felt that my blood was having a hard time making it back to my heart and unfortunately, had stopped taking suggestions from my brain. Heavy pelting rain flooded the sloping driveway, entered the garage and seeped into the ground*

floor where I had camped out. Bravely and stupidly, I donned my raingear, disengaged and slid open the overhead garage door, went outside and started clearing the clogged drain that was responsible for the wayward flow of the water. Along came a gust of wind and the garage door slammed shut. I was locked out. Standing knee-deep in water and being pelted with 150mph winds, I was facing at least 24 hours of extreme physical and emotional Stress. A slow dash to a hideaway beneath some concrete steps was my initial plan. With protection on three sides only, water soon invaded and the zone had to be evacuated. In the low visibility from blistering rain, I managed to reach the hillside gazebo to search for the extra key to the plant nursey, some 50 yards away. The wooden drawer that held the key had collapsed and the key had been blown over the edge of the railing. The yellow rubber band to which the key was attached was visible on the side of the hill. Adrenalin pumping and cortisol nearing maximum levels (whatever they were), I climbed down the side of the hill, secured the key, and made my way along the embankment toward the greenhouse to avoid being struck by flying debris. It took a second lifetime to reach the nursery and get inside to the concrete bathroom that at least was dry and apparently, "safe". Now completely in survival mode and realizing there was no food and questionable contaminated water to last for the next 24 hours. Switching to "wait it out" mode where emotional stress takes over from the physical, I began to implement my basic strategies for stress control. Plan, organize, purpose, meditate, relax, sleep, wake, then plan some more. The 69 year old male in fairly good health, came through the storm with determination to repair damaged farm that itself had had a purpose, that of healing, and then pursue the quest for a stress-free life of creativity, discovery and progress. Adherence to the 6 basic strategies of a stress free life, nutrition, exercise, mental stimulation, social connections, avoidance of toxins, and specific techniques for stress control would become my direct routing to a goal of happiness. Having been joined by my wife a week after the ordeal, the strength of my plan became complete.

On the other hand, another 69 year old male who rode out the storm inside hurricane proof house, with minimal damage to surroundings, had no plan, no stress control, no clear understanding of what had happened, alone with only negative thoughts, and an "Oh Shit" attitude, emerged sick and in shock and facing months of no electricity, poor food intake, no joy in life, no relief on sight, was hospitalized on a slew of pharmaceuticals, and lingered near death for months, before finally succumbing to stroke and total organ shutdown.

Having had the opportunity and good fortune to have travelled and observed the processes and effects of stress, both environmental and emotional, differences in outcomes from availability of adequate nutrition, physical activity, mental stimulation (education), low stress, social interactions, and toxins exposure, directly influence life results as to which become successes or failures, and ultimately determine good or poor health. "Stress, depression, domestic violence, and bullying appear to be the rule rather than the exception." Karen Gaskell in *Dark Side of America.*

In Africa, the Caribbean, South America and Asia, lives in poverty with lack of basic amenities, access to opportunities, reflect in lack of basic courtesies, unhappiness and compromised productivity. Lives in the United States of America for non-whites, where the basic amenities, educational and job opportunities, and basic dignity are deliberately withheld through profiling and hatred without due cause, suffer the mental and physical stresses that translate directly to poor health. Poverty and racism are directly contributory to keeping USA statistics below those of the rest of the developed world. Stress of distrust, hatred, prospective violence, and daily discourtesies are directly linked to high disease incidence and prevalence.

To achieve a status of good health, physically, emotionally and spiritually, one must be essentially free of stress, or at a level of control of the stress response that blocks most or all of the biochemical and physiological damaging results.

> *"All living things encounter stress in one form or another; microbes, plants and animals, and develop mechanisms to avoid and cope, to ensure survival."*
>
> A.L. ANDUZE

Statistics

STRESS is associated with 70 to 80% of physician visits in the USA. Primary causes associated with anxiety and stress, secondary associated with musculoskeletal issues and accounts for $300 billion in annual costs to employers in missed work and health care.

18% of the USA adult population experiences hospital-grade anxiety-related issues.
45% of crimes committed are associated with mental health issues associated with stress.

USA spends the highest % of GDP on health care, yet has the lowest life expectancy and "sickest" people of the developed/industrial countries. It has the highest disease prevalence of the basic chronic diseases: heart (hypertension & stroke), cancer, diabetes, and neurodegenerative diseases. All are stress related. As the USA has the highest stress-induced population it is #1 in stress –related diseases. WHY? A society that does not take care of one another, that is selfish and maintains an every man for himself daily routine, winner-take-all ideology, yields a scramble for life, creating unbelievable daily stressors for the majority of its population.

Urban vs rural life, inner city strife, poor nutrition even among middle and upper middle class populations, deprivation of exposure to and interaction with "others", inadequate housing, daily insults, confinement (lack of access to the world, to meaningful information), a daily struggle for basic amenities, lack of basic education about healthy nutrition and lifestyle, lead to stress related conditions of obesity, diabetes, hypertension, inflammation diseases, mental instability, death by alcohol, accident, and homicide. Unfortunately, being on 2 to 3 medications daily has become accepted as the "normal".

USA health response policy is one of pushing opioids and painkillers and antidepressants and sedatives to address stress related issues. A healthy 60 year old adult is the exception not the rule.

1 in 6 Americans has taken psychiatric psychotropic psychoactive drug as antidepressant or sedative in the past year. Deaths by drugs, alcohol, and suicide are soaring. 2 out of 3 individuals over the age of 50 are reliant on one or more medications in order to function at a basal level.

In Britain: 1 in 3 sick notes are for mental health issues. Depression, stress-related problems, and bereavement are listed as most common reasons for sick note.

In USA: there are 4.5 million deaths per year due to pollution and toxins in an environment closely linked to a carbon-intensive economy.

1. 77% of Americans regularly experience chronic stress (physical)
2. 73% of Americans regularly experience emotional stress
3. 33% (1 in 3) feel they are living with extreme daily stress
4. 48% feel that their stress levels increased in past 5 years
5. 76% cited finances and work as chief causes of stress
6. 48% lose sleep at night due to stress related issues
7. 48% say that stress affects their personal & professional lives (dysfunction)

The acceptance of preventable debilitating diseases is astounding. Treatment with pharmaceuticals is the normal response to the presence of stress-related diseases. This book attempts to understand and provide a route by which one can control the stress response and reduce the risk of succumbing to any of these chronic diseases. There are 3 processes: understand the concept of stress, how use techniques and strategies to control the stress response and how to avoid stress all together.

The definition of Stress: *A state of mental tension and worry caused by problems in your life, work, etc. or something that causes strong feelings of worry or anxiety, be it a physical force or pressure.* (Merriam-Webster Dictionary). A Stressor is a challenging or threatening event, item or situation existing that leads to a stress response. Stress elicits the release of stress hormones, led by cortisol, adrenaline, norepinephrine…that can damage the cells and tissues of the body.

Chapter one may be a bit medical and overly technical, which serves to demonstrate how variable and complicated the stress response really is. An adequate understanding of the basics of the stress hormone release mechanisms and how the body and mind are affected; is essential to being able to manage the stress response.

Causes of Stress: May be *external* (environmental, heat, cold, pollution, toxins, radiation, too much, too little or *internal*: the stressor generating a response may be external or internal, physical or emotional... but the response is always biochemical, physiological and real.

Of the modernized industrialized advanced countries, USA is near the bottom of the list in terms of health of its population. Though some blame can be placed on the for-profit Health Care system that puts profit ahead of patient care and largely ignores preventive care, optimal health will never be achieved until more emphasis is placed on the six basic strategies of good health: exercise, healthy nutrition, meaningful social interactions, mental stimulation, effective stress control and avoidance of toxins and toxic environments.

The American diet is atrocious, consisting largely of high fat, high protein, food additives, and artificial foods grown with chemicals. The reliance on supermarkets instead of local markets with affordable organically grown products is a major factor in physical stress on the body. Very little effort is made in consciously selecting food to consume that is devoid of toxic chemicals. The results are evident in the degree of obesity and inflammation present in the population.

The lack of exercise mainly in cities that are ill-suited for walking or cycling, coupled with the lack of initiative to become and stay physically active is a major factor in poor mental and physical health. Heart disease, poor circulation and inadequate immune systems result from this omission.

Mental stimulation is severely lacking. Americans do not read. The literacy rate is lower than expected. Meaningless TV programs, inane videos and electronic games, which are mostly violent and supplant basic reading. The general lack of knowledge of the world, its geopolitics; the lack of language skills, abhorrence and avoidance of "others" different than oneself or immediate group, is shameful.

Social Connections are almost nonexistent, as Americans fear and hate each other, as well as anyone considered as foreign. Dining is a private matter, gated communities, barbed wire, exultation in fences and walls to keep people out, fear and ignorance of others, lead to solitude, loneliness and illness. The high percentage of people who live alone out of choice and out of necessity is connected to poor health and a failing society.

Stress levels are extremely high in a winner-take-all society in which hatred and interpersonal relationships are awful, and competitive rivalry is encouraged in the name of productivity and success. The emotional stress that is inflicted is addressed to a large extent by drugs (legal & illegal) as an easy solution to all problems. In the face of overwhelming stress, coping mechanisms, ranging from meditation and music to marijuana and frequent sex, are available, while prevention measures are largely ignored.

Risky behavior and exposure to toxins are extremely high. Poisons in the air, the emissions from fossil fuels, contaminated food and water, household materials, lead to a chemical environment that is not conducive with good health.

The USA is lacking in all six categories of health maintenance (when compared to other developed countries), so the health care system really doesn't matter ... the basic health is poor and worsening. In the so-called blue zones (Dan Buettner), successful longevity is reliant on good health through adherence to all six of the basic strategies. Societies in which the citizens are unhappy, angry, mean and cruel to each other as well as to others usually harbor people in poor health and with shortened lifespans.

Of the six basic strategies to healthy Lifestyle, *the key to good health is Stress Control*. Excess stress on a chronic level leads to mind and body dysfunction and illness. After a visit to Ikaria, a Greek island in the Aegean Sea, and interaction with a significant portion of the population, I am convinced that the key to longevity is to avoid getting stress-related diseases in the first place.

The quantity and quality of the threat/ Stressor is insignificant when compared to the individual's response to it. There is an over-reaction (pop a pill) and under-reaction (ignore, internalize or pray).

In modern times, crucial to the successful management of stress is the understanding that it is a real entity with chemical and physiological components that can and will result in dysfunction and permanent damage that is real. It can also be faced head on, avoided, and managed by coping strategies.

Diseases of Stress: In his classic book, *The Stress of Life*, the pioneer of stress physiology, Hans Selye, MD, presents his definition of stress in terms of its association with disease. Acute stress is necessary for the organism to thrive, while chronic stress leads to debilitation through inflammation, disease and eventual organ failure. My mentor and pioneer in Integrative Medicine, Professor Andrew Weil, MD, takes it to another level. The clinical association of stress with practical life, the identification of stress and the management techniques should be incorporated in everyday medical practice and with every patient. In doing this in my practice, I found that almost all glaucoma, arthritis, diabetic retinopathy, hypertension, cancer and neurodegenerative diseases are associated with some level of stress linked to inflammation and naturally resulting in a high prevalence of morbidity and debilitation.

Stress Response & Management: Comprise a complex set of cause/effect events, consisting of a stressor, real or perceived as in a challenge or threat and *a chemical response (release of stress hormones), that leads to physiological metabolic reaction.* How this response is processed, determines the intermediate effect on the individual and the ultimate response. This response may consist of several varying reactions individually of in concert with one another. First there is Acceptance, allowing the stress reaction to take its toll, and taking no action or willingly enduring the consequences; second is Adaptation, wherein coping techniques are called upon to reduce the reaction; third is Alteration, which is an attempt to change the stressor and the response to make them easier to endure; and fourth is Avoidance, getting rid of the stressor altogether, so minimal or no response would be necessary.

The focus of this book is to examine the last of these responses, Avoidance, by which the individual gets rid of the stressor or prevents the response. Through the creation of a personal blue zone, in which the individual functions in a healthy environment, enabling stressors and stress responses can be minimized. Though it must be emphasized that a life without stress is impossible, a life filled with stress is not necessary.

The following is my personal Stress-free Life protocol according to the six basic strategies for good health.

GOOD HEALTH & A STRONG IMMUNE SYSTEM ARE THE KEYS TO SUCCESSFUL STRESS CONTROL.

Follow the Six Basic Strategies of Good Health for longevity and high quality of life:

1. Exercise: get moving, keep moving, strengthen the immune system, all organs, and muscles
2. Nutrition: balanced diet, good food, organic, local, portion size, weight control
3. Social Connections: trusted friendships, inclusion, shared events
4. Mental Stimulation: purpose, goals, organization, learning
5. Stress management: positive outlook, reduce inflammation, maintain natural hormonal metabolism, relaxation
6. Avoid toxins, pollutants, and bad habits,

Each strategy influences and is heavily influenced by the other. From *Natural Health & Disease Prevention,* 2016, Alfred L. Anduze, MD

This is a *How to book,* which is based on suggestions from other referenced books, medical knowledge concerning the results of chronic stress, and personal efforts to reduce stress levels. Many volumes and articles on stress push one towards group sessions, personal psychological therapy, biofeedback mechanisms and conventional medications, which are inappropriate for the average person in the average neighborhood. This book attempts to address the stressors of the average daily life and suggest viable, realistic strategies for successful management. In the art and science of medicine, the best remedies involve attention to and understanding of the cause or causes of disease. Similarly, the stress-free life protocol that follows contains suggestions for the management of stress that are simple and that work. Simply identify the stressor and choose which responses are best suited to your situation.

How the downtrodden deal with the stress of daily living in Haiti, Bangladesh, and many areas of Sub-Saharan Africa; how the physically challenged deal with their disabilities in a world that often ignores them; how the environmentally disadvantaged deal with chronic recurrent stress (earthquakes in Mexico, Peru and Ecuador, Italy, and Indonesia and tsunamis, famines, droughts, floods, and hurricanes in the Caribbean, is the real subject of this book.

Consciously, focus and re-focus, get in touch with yourself and set up your own protocol for a Stress-free Life Plan, directed at reducing your stress level by adopting the basic elements of the other five strategies, and achieving a state of good health and wellbeing.

> *"In life, we lurch from one crisis to another, rarely solving, more often barely coping and then succumbing, but never really entirely free from stress."*
>
> A. L. ANDUZE, 1990, *MUSINGS*

My Personal STRESS-FREE LIFE Protocol

1. STRESS CONTROL: Positive Outlook, Journaling, Organize your time; Plan, set a Purpose, Meaning, have a Goal; Work-life balance, Stay in the present & look to the future; Music, Expressive Art therapy, Breathing techniques, Regular sex, Aromatherapy.

2. EXERCISE: Walk 30 minutes a day, 4 days a week; Yoga, Tai chi, weight training, aerobics exercise, bike-Treadmill (3 days a week), vigorous dance, hillside gardening, (daily).

3. NUTRITION: Balanced Diet, local organic food, fresh vegetables, fruit and grains; Weight control; Vitamins B complex and C, Adaptogens (Siberian ginseng, Rhodiolarosea or Schizandra) 2 or 3 times a week.

Lemongrass, lemon-balm, &mint as Herbal teas (relaxation inducers). Ginger & Turmeric in cooking (daily to prevent inflammation); Dark chocolate square as evening reward.

4. SOCIAL CONNECTIONS: Trusted friends, laughter, regular visits, share experiences, share meals, media connections and face-to-face daily.

5. MENTAL STIMULATION: Learn new things, Travel, explore, Exercise the brain (read, puzzles, study, write), Relaxation, Meditation, Quality Sleep, Rejuvenation.

6. AVOID excesses: Moderate alcohol (red wine), no smoking, no legal or illegal drugs, no toxin exposure (environmental air pollution, plastics, foils, fertilizers, pesticides...). Know your limits (age related behavior).

Alfred L. Anduze, MD, age 70

CHAPTER ONE
BIOCHEMISTRY AND PHYSIOLOGY OF STRESS

Key Words: Stressor, cortisol & epinephrine, dopamine & serotonin, symptoms of stress, Hypothalamus-Pituitary-Adrenal axis and Sympatho-Medullary Systems, inflammation, feel good hormones; feel bad hormones, measuring stress levels.

"Stress is the non-specific response of the body to any demand...

Stress is such that poverty and starvation can elicit similar response as extreme wealth (fear of loss) and overeating... Stress is real and causes changes in structure and chemical composition of the body, some damage, some building...

General Adaptation Syndrome (GAS) consists of (1) alarm reaction (2) stage of resistance and (3) stage of exhaustion."
HANS SELYE, MD, HUNGARIAN-CANADIAN ENDOCRINOLOGIST, 1907-1982, RECOGNIZED AS THE FIRST TO DEMONSTRATE THE EXISTENCE OF BIOLOGICAL STRESS.

1

"Stressed- out is when you start getting on your own nerves".

The Science of Stress

S TRESS is an organism's response to a stressor (a threat), which may be external or internal, physical or emotional, environmental or personal. Stress may come in the form of heat or cold, natural disasters, feasts or famines. There is a cause and effect (relationship) involving the biochemical and physiological consequences of external and internal factors that stimulate the Sympathetic Nervous System to release hormones associated with metabolic reactions that can be beneficial or detrimental. The mind, body and spirit response may be one of challenge or neglect with which the organism reacts. Stress takes the organism out of its comfort zone of hemostasis, and the resultant struggle is for complete recovery. It is a real entity, powerful, consequential and is often the determining factor of the state of health of the organism. (Author's summary)

"When stress is at its highest, just know that it can only go down, or, you can implode and simply have a melt-down, or better yet, explode and take some people with you"

A.L. ANDUZE, MD

Biology, Chemistry & Physiology of Stress (stressor & response)

When you feel "stressed out" your brain is pumping out stress hormones which are crashing into receptors and knocking all the good stuff out of the way. Then it sends out a damage report. Anxiously, you wait for the recovery, but it doesn't come. Instead, a more formal message arrives. Another set of high powered stress hormones are being released into the blood stream and are on route to the brain. When this scenario is repeated and sustained for months to years, disease enters and eventually dominates the picture.

Stress is a normal part of biological existence. All living things undergo and experience "stress", such as attacks by pathogens, climate, success and failure in nourishment, shelter and natural interactions. The nature of one's reaction determines the outcome.

Humans still have the same genes as they did 20,000 years ago. We are designed to react to storms, run from lions, summon the energy and skill to capture our food and defend our territory. The physical stressors that elicit an appropriate acute reaction also allow us to achieve positive recovery time. In modern times, the environmental stressors have coupled with emotional stressors. Together, when they become chronic, in the absence of recovery, they cause more permanent damages to the body, mind and spirit.

Stress-Response Mechanism

STRESSOR (emotional/physical) ->>> Stress Hormones release (chronicity) -> -> ->Inflammation + Oxidative stress (free radical DNA damage & disruption of repair) -> -> ->Toxic body

3

and mind -> -> -> more Stress response (emotional) -> -> -> more stressor ->-> ->More stress hormones release -> -> -> toxicity -> -> accelerated ageing & tissue breakdown ->DISEASE

Symptoms of Chronic Stress Response are weight loss, headache, decreased appetite, neck pain, heart palpitations, insomnia, anxiety, anger, weakness, irritability, depression and heartburn. The butterflies in your stomach before a big speech, or before a life-changing exam are related to an excess amount of cortisol. Similarly, the excitement before a big trip, before a wedding, after receiving applause, getting a promotion or meeting a new love are related to cortisol. The crash in your stomach after losing your job, losing a big bet, losing a great love, receiving an unexpected huge bill, being passed up for promotion, or stuck in traffic and past deadline time to arrive, are related to cortisol. This is the *same chemical acting on different receptors to give different responses.* One is normal Eustress which is positive and constructive and the other is Distress, which is negative and can be destructive.

Vignette #2: *"I love the kind of hugs where you can physically feel the sadness leaving your body."* Charles M Schulz (1922-2000), endorsed by my good friend, T.E. Highfield

A stressor agent is one that produces stress. Stress is the reaction to a stressor(s), which may be mental or physical, internal or external, personal or environmental. Plants and trees have stress; react to it positively or negatively, depending on their health and predicament. The stress response may be the same whether the stressor is pleasant or unpleasant, may differ depending on the situation such as duration and intensity of the stressor, or the physical and mental health of the recipient.

The Stress response is characterized by the activity of *feel-good and feel- bad hormones,* whose resulting action depends on the characteristics of the situation that elicited the response.

Feel-Good Hormones
dopamine, oxytocin, serotonin, endorphins, melatonin,
phenylethylamine, ghrelin

Feel-Bad Hormones
cortisol, norepinephrine, epinephrine, hydrogen ions as
free radicals, reactive oxygen
species,

For example, serotonin may completely neutralize the inflammatory activity of cortisol, or may itself be completely overwhelmed and neutralized by the same number one stress hormone.

Hans Selye, MD

In his discovery of 1936 that rats respond to various damaging stimuli with a general response that involves alarm, resistance and exhaustion, Dr. Selye defined Stress as "the nonspecific response of the body to any demand". Alarm is the initial response in the fight or flight response; Resistance is a period in which the body adapts to repeated exposure to the stress; and Exhaustion is a relapse in symptoms that occurs when the stress is exerted for too long. He labelled it this phenomenon as the GAS syndrome, which described immune system suppression, ulceration of the lining of the stomach and small intestine as a result of acidic bombardment, and activation of two major stress response pathways.

When an animal is confronted with a stressful situation, stress hormones act together to increase glucose levels in the blood for the purpose of providing energy for the body to react. This reaction may be positive, as in fight or flight, or destructive, as in the onset and promotion of inflammatory disease processes. In plants, stressors may be related to drought, flood, windstorm, earthquake, changes in soil chemistry (oxygen and nitrogen levels), quantity & quality, disease and pests, mechanical injuries, root injuries, whether the tree is solitary or in forest, and result in an increase or decrease in medicinal production, varying rates of photosynthesis and transpiration, wilting, overgrowth, reduced vigor, and eventual premature death.

The Stress Response may be Acute or Chronic

"Stress is like spice - in the right proportion it enhances the flavor of the dish. Too little produces a bland, dull meal; Too much may choke you."

DONALD TUBESING

Stress may be acute as in bad events, insults, and challenging situations or chronic as in repeated assaults and arguments which cause a steady release of stress hormones. The primary response is usually the same stimulation of the HPA axis that results in the release of cortisol, norepinephrine, and other stress hormones, with a coinciding release of multiple hormones from adrenal glands, thymus and stomach. The Acute response is short term and stimulates the appropriate inflammatory pathways to elicit a positive eventual healing effect toward full recovery. It is good in that a small amount and at regular frequencies is required to keep defensive hormones regulated and keep the immune system sharp and on alert. Acute stress has meaning and purpose and is an asset to the wellbeing of the organism. Some like warriors, corporate types and assassins revel in this type of the stress response. In anticipation of the "rush", they seek situations that create stress in order to precipitate the experience repeatedly and likewise, the recovery is taken as relief.

The Chronic response results in a steady release of stress hormones which is varies in intensity, is frequent, repetitive and whose inflammation response is more damaging than that of the acute response. Over time, it wears the organism down and may lead to disease.

"Pain that has no meaning becomes suffering... while pain with a purpose becomes noble...like pain transferred to spiritual level... suffering for redemption or repentance (results in) achievement of purity," is a statement from Dr Amit Sood, 2013, in his Mayo Clinic, *Guide to Stress free Living.*

In 1936, Dr. Selye's rats responded to damaging stimuli with alarm, resistance, & exhaustion (ARE). A for alarm, leading to flight or fight; R for resistance, leading to adaptation to repeated exposure to same stimuli, which resulted in eventual numbness; and E for exhaustion, leading to collapse of the organism when the exposure was prolonged. This he termed Biological Stress, as the physiological response of an organism to stressful stimuli, which involved genetics such as DNA programming, endocrinology and brain imaging.

Stress Response at the Chemical Level

The two major Stress Response Systems, HPA axis (Hypothalamus-Pituitary-Adrenal), endocrine produces cortisol, and the Sympathetic Nervous System, autonomic, produces norepinephrine and epinephrine, also known as noradrenalin and adrenalin Both result in physical (cardiovascular and physiological) reactions as well as psychological/emotional reactions. The Stress Response begins when a stressor stimulates the hypothalamus in the brain to secrete (1) corticotropin-releasing hormone (CTR), which causes the pituitary gland to release (2) adrenocorticotropic hormone (ACTH), which stimulates the adrenal gland to release cortisol, norepinephrine (NE), serotonin (S) and Neuropeptide Y (NPY), from the brain (hypothalamus, amygdala, hippocampus, prefrontal cortex, locus coeruleus, raphe nucleus) and spinal cord. In the acute response, actin release leads to recovery and in the chronic response, cortisol leads to the steady release of glucose into the blood stream and tissues, which causes the inflammation, anxiety, depression, weight gain or loss, and eventual illnesses. CORTISOL is the main stress hormone and is made from cholesterol in the adrenal cortex and the liver. You can "feel its release" as surges of dread, instant waves of weakness, and "bad feeling" nausea and quasi-nausea. With normal cortisol metabolism, there is a regular release in the mid-morning, around 10 to 11 a.m. and again around 4 to 6 pm; a release with exercise; a release with acute stress which leads to recovery and a release with chronic stress which lingers and is steady or comes in bursts and accumulates.

The release of cortisol and epinephrine from the adrenal glands leads to preparation for the use of muscle energy. This requires excess glucose and reduced insulin in order to keep glucose around for instant and prolonged utilization. The individual experiences an increase in heart rate, sweating, and muscle readiness until a return to "normal" after the stressor is reduced or eliminated. The healthy acute response of alarm and resistance ends in recovery. The chronic response is the one that is always with you, that you can't get rid of, that leads to exhaustion and inflammation.

Cortisol, aldosterone, and cortisone are pro-inflammation stress hormones from the adrenal cortex when chronic, and anti-inflammation when acute. Mineralocorticoids may be pro-inflammatory and glucocorticoids may be anti-inflammatory, depending on the nature, timing, frequency, duration and intensity of the stressor and on the health status of the recipient. Overproduction or prolonged release or any and all of these hormones may lead to an overwhelming of the adrenal glands (Adrenal Fatigue),which leads to further overproduction of stress hormones, and subsequent damage to end organs and tissues.

Excess cortisol weakens the immune system by preventing the normal proliferation of T-cells, which leads to further disruption in the production of essential cellular components. In an adverse stress response from an excess release of stress hormones, there is an "overreaction" in which more energy is expended than replaced. This depletion of energy reserves leads to a dysfunctional immune system response which may be seen as an inappropriate emotional or physical response.

Studies on stress response levels confirm the effect on biochemical and physiological metabolism. For example, just writing expressions of love and affection can lead to a reduction in cholesterol levels in the blood in healthy adults. The recall of an adverse stressor can result in a rise in blood pressure. The anticipation and expression of laughter reduces blood levels of stress hormones (cortisol and adrenaline) and laughing at a funny movie increases beta-endorphins involved in mood elevation and human growth hormone (HGH) and leads to better sleep and cellular repair.

Cortisol and other stress hormones, when released in large amounts, frequently and for long periods of time can result in cell, tissue and organ damage.

Stress Response at the Cellular Level

The HPS axis and Sympathetic Autonomic Nervous System react to stressors and produce hormones which result in the biochemical and physiological tissue effects we recognize as Stress. DNA mitochondria in a person's cells, that normally produce energy, are rendered dysfunctional by excess cortisol. Energy needed for normal function of basal metabolism is lacking.

In acute stress, the response is a cellular inflammation consisting of cytokines, tumor necrosis factor, interleukins, IL-1 and IL-6 and chemokines that lead to the release T-killer cells whose job is to get rid of pathogens and initiate constructive healing. This production of killer cells and cytokines are at high levels in order to signal the brain that the body is sick. The subsequent reaction of fever, energy loss, and appetite suppression, has a positive function of fighting pathogens and initiating healing. Similar responses will also work for stressful events, like important exams, life changing events (family death, divorce, loss of normalcy), but they are characterized by a return to normalcy.

In chronic stress, with repeated exposure to stressors of longer duration and variable intensity, this same mechanism, with some changes, leads to a destructive inflammation that has long term damage to tissues and resultant interruption of function. There is a slow, repeated release of cortisol, and other stress hormones, which leads to cell membrane and DNA injury, and the release of free radicals from and into cells. This is the *oxidative stress* responsible for the low grade inflammation that we see in some heart disease, hypertension (HBP), gastrointestinal disorders, diabetes, liver and kidney diseases, arthritis, dementia, neurodegenerative diseases, and cancer. There is an increase in the stress index score resulting in a greater severity of cold symptoms and increased speed of viral progression as seen in HIV studies. There is a faster progression and decreased survival rates with just about all cancers.

This inflammation is often interconnected with obesity and low insulin sensitivity and high resistance, and leads to damage to imbalances in metabolic function and damage to all components of the cell. With prolonged release of cortisol and epinephrine, there is an increased formation of oxygen free radicals (as O instead of O2), which damages organ systems and leads to premature ageing. Oxygen in moderation and in proper structure gives life and in excess or improper structure, brings death faster. Abnormal glucose and poor protein synthesis leads to immune system breakdown, which is manifested in a toxic liver, inflamed colon, joint pain and the release of lactic acid, and other pro-inflammation chemicals that promote INFLAMMATION.

Malfunction of the cells in choosing sugar fermentation over oxygen for respiration is accompanied by a dysfunctional immune system that offers no defense against environmental conditions and toxins, and leaves the individual more susceptible to disease. Most illnesses, like infections and cancer, are due to a combination of exposure to toxins and an unhealthy cellular matrix plus stress-induced inflammation. This leads to further cellular impairment through DNA and cell membrane injury, oxidative stress, shutdown of the parasympathetic system, prolonged sympathetic (ANS) system and hypothalamic-pituitary-adrenal (HPA) system overproduction and overuse of energy without proper replenishment.

Physiology of the Acute
Physical Stress Response

1. Increased heart rate, pulse and blood pressure intended to send more blood/energy to muscles and nerves needed for "action"
2. Brain takes in more oxygen in a state of lightheaded, unfocused thinking of fight or flight
3. Pupils dilate to admit more light
4. Nose and throat widen to permit more air flow
5. Saliva secretion shuts down leading in dry mouth
6. Lungs take in more oxygen leading to dilated bronchi, hyperventilation, shaky voice
7. Peripheral vasoconstriction redirects blood to muscles and internal organs)
8. Increased skeletal muscle tension (O2 from lungs & sugar from cortisol are pumped to muscles)
9. Liver releases more sugar into the blood for energy for muscles & brain
10. Digestive system shuts down to divert energy to lungs, heart, muscles giving a queasy feeling
11. "Cold" sweat, body heats up from reaction and sweats to cool itself down
12. Immune system function efficiency decreases, bone marrow produces more white blood cells, which give more inflammatory reaction, which, when chronic and repeated results in a grinding down effect leading to illness
13. Spleen releases more red blood cells to bring more oxygen to tissues
14. Adrenal glands release more adrenalin which raises the BP, heart rate, fatty acids and sugar in blood stream even more.

Physiology of the Chronic Physical Stress Response

1. Back, neck and chest pain, headache (tension)
2. Diaphoresis (cold sweats, hot sweats)
3. Obesity (related to inflammation, and/or compensatory eating; or weight loss)
4. Erectile dysfunction, reduced libido, cramps,
5. Syncope (fainting spells)
6. Heart palpitations, arrhythmias,
7. Anxiety, nervous tics, panic attacks
8. Insomnia
9. Digestive issues, appetite loss, heartburn, GI reflux disorder
10. Difficulty fighting off or recovery from disease.

Physiology of the Chronic Mental Stress Response

1. Anxiety, irritability, anger
2. Depression (inflammation related)
3. Burnout
4. Sadness
5. Forgetful
6. Poor concentration, poor focus
7. Insecurity, restlessness.

Behavioral Effects of Stress

1. Compensatory alcohol, drugs, cigarettes, high caffeine intake
2. Search for relief (drugs, legal & illegal)

3. Bowel issues
4. Recurrent headaches
5. Family conflicts
6. Work issues
7. Relationships damaged/compromised
8. Self-mutilation
9. Suicide
10. Social isolation.

In the 21st century, most threats are social (emotional) not physical, and prolonged states of stress involve the brain and its relation to and control of the body. The chemical and cellular responses that were developed to contribute to the survival and preservation of the organism may ultimately cause its demise when overloaded.

Types of Stress

Stressors can be places, objects, persons, or situations that trigger or lead to the stress response.

Acute stress occurs when a direct challenge, event or demand triggers the Central Nervous System and endocrine glands to release hormones to target organs, resulting in anxiety, changes in vital signs, rises in blood sugar, changes in blood flow dynamics, intended to increase energy expenditure and facilitate the fight or flight offensive or defensive action, such as occurs in a heated argument, a near miss accident, a victim of crime. Upon the appropriate signal, all returns to the homeostatic normal.

Episodic acute stress takes a bit longer, has less of a time interval, and results in an irritable, anxious, pessimistic, negative behavior with a personality that tends to accept stress as normal.

Chronic stress is more constant and persistent, such as occurs with poverty, a dysfunctional family, an unhappy marriage, and a bad job. It takes a higher toll on the individual, resulting in hypertension, increased risk of stroke, heart attack, vulnerability to anxiety and depression, infertility, and an increase in rate of ageing. Cortisol is overproduced resulting in lower cytokines production which leads to fewer receptors available on immune cells, such that when stress occurs in waves the inflammation continues indefinitely.

Oxidative stress occurs when the organism fails to detoxify reactive oxygen species (ROS) from toxins generated internally and externally from excesses or deficiencies or to repair the resulting damages. It occurs at the cellular level and is associated with regular and accelerated ageing and many chronic debilitating diseases.

Pathology of the Stress Response

The human cell has telomeres, protective caps at ends of each DNA chromosome strand. As oxidative stress increases, so does the level of telomere activity leading to a shortening of telomere length. As it is "used up", the cell "ages". Chronic stress leads to increased rate of ageing.

Communities and societies with the least stress have the lowest rates of ageing and highest longevity (Blue Zones). It is the response to a stressor (any demand) that determines the effect on the mind, body and spirit. A poor stress response leads to poor health, which is a major impediment to longevity.

Immune system dysfunction is the main reason for an increased susceptibility to acute physical illnesses such as the common cold, flu infections, allergies, neurological diseases, autoimmune disorders, delayed and incomplete wound healing, cardiovascular and endocrine dysfunction, and digestive ailments like indigestion and mal-absorption. Low grade inflammations are associated with chronic illnesses like arthritis, gastritis, enteritis, hepatitis, pancreatitis, neuropathies, cancer, stroke, lung disease, diabetes, accidents, liver cirrhosis, and suicide.

Organ dysfunction is associated with Metabolic Syndrome (hypertension, elevated triglycerides/decreased high density lipoproteins (HDL) and diabetes (insulin resistance& impaired glucose tolerance).

Obesity, characterized by the accumulation of brown fat, (visceral) waist fat in men, and thigh and hip fat in women, contributes to the hormonal and metabolic changes in heart disease, arthritis, fibromyalgia, body inflammation breakdown due to oxidative stress of cellular dysfunctions and eventual organ damage resulting in premature death.

Mental health impairment such as in clinical depression, anxiety and post-traumatic stress disorder (PTSD), sometimes displays a lack of sufficient brain chemicals, like gamma-aminobutyric acid (GABA) and serotonin, and a physical change in brain anatomy due to the formation of tangles and accumulation of beta-amyloid. There is a depletion of body energy, low grade inflammation, and a lack of effective coping mechanisms in place, in a situation that persists over long periods of time, such as observed in individuals residing in dangerous or poor neighborhoods or subjected to humiliation on a daily basis.

Conditions like Alzheimer's dementia can be linked to exposure to air and food pollutants, heavy metals and high cortisol levels, which are directly related to a deterioration of the hippocampus of the brain and a resultant decline of memory. The effect of a poor environment and high stress on a healthy individual with immune system intact may be one of partial suppression of cellular and humoral function in addition to a low-grade, non-specific chronic inflammation. The effect on an immunocompromised individual is one of full blown inflammation leading to illness. High Cortisol levels lead to changes in behavior and physiology. A harsh environment (physical or emotional) such as one of extreme cold or heat, prolonged darkness or extreme light, with high exposure to pollutants and toxins, wears down the defenses of the mind, body and spirit.

Clinical Reactions to Excess Stress Hormones

With acute stressors and a good release, there is energy for action or repair, with eventual recovery and return to normal. With a bad release, a panic attack may occur with shortness of breath, numbness and tingling in the extremities, chest pain, nausea, anxiety, nervousness, a sense of impending doom, and inability to cope, accompanied by increased heart rate and blood pressure, and anger. The reactions maybe appear right away or are held in for weeks, which may lead to depression and insomnia, and get progressively better or worse.

With chronic stressors, most often the initial release is bad and becomes characterized by recurrent bursts or steady release of stress hormones, which promote oxidative stress with its release of free radicals that cause irreversible cellular damage. In many cases, chronic stress leads to a stability of the stress response that becomes the "new normal". The individual and the society accept these levels of stress as they know nothing else. Those living with poverty, racism, and discrimination show an adjustment to humiliation, insults and to daily stressors. Young black men as victims of police brutality, with incarceration as a way of life, and a given destiny of failure, express themselves in ways that are often counteractive. Their levels of glaucoma, hypertension and death by trauma, far outstrip those of the old normal.

In the fifteenth century when the Europeans went to Africa, North and South America and Asia promoting trade and procuring obscene wealth, they brought their fears and sense of entitlement to these lands and imposed them upon the minds and bodies of all indigenous people. It was a sense that no matter what beliefs they held or what they had accomplished was only deserving of humiliation, destruction and permanent second class status or death. This sense of defeat and permanent lowly status in society, subject to daily insults and striving without reward (or jumping up to reach bottom), is a burden of chronic stress that generates a constant stream of hormones that keeps the mind and body in a state of constant imbalance. When expected to perform, create and produce at the same level of those who have assumed the roles of privilege, biochemically and physiologically, it becomes difficult and leads to chronic stress.

Perceived Reactions to the Stress Response

When under stress, one feels the emptiness in the pit of the stomach, blanching of the skin and reduced blood flow, nausea and unsteadiness, the need to make a fist or flail the arms to run away. These feelings are present whether it is in response to an argument, a threat, a challenge, a sudden love interest or a love rejection, and loss, leading to loneliness and or homelessness. It is the same release and effects of the accumulation of cortisol and other stress hormones.

Measuring Stress Levels and Reactions

Measurements of the stress response can be done by several techniques. Cortisol and alpha-amylase levels as biochemical indicators of presence and degree of Sympathetic Nervous System (SNS) activity can be measured via markers in the saliva of animals. Levels of epinephrine and norepinephrine in the blood, brain derived neurotrophic factor (BDNF), reactive oxygen species (ROS) levels in microorganisms, ring scoring in trees, and various ultrasonic, diffraction and chemical assays are some of the more common stress markers. The amount of stress to which an individual is subjected over time plus frequency, duration and intensity, can be quantified by measuring effects on the organ systems to arrive at a "Stress Index" that is standardized to fit most biological models.

Through surveys, the subjective response level to a particular event may be graded. An individual reaction to the stressor may consist of a) panic and scream, b) hold in and boil, c) ignore, and d) accept and cope. The intensity of the responses can be noted and compared.

Through a blood test of C-reactive protein levels (CRP) and homocysteine levels, the presence and amount of inflammation and toxicity can be measured in human subjects.

A study ascertaining stress levels in elephants was done by measuring the levels of glucocorticosteroid chemicals in their fecal matter or blood samples. The causes were noted as related to predators, food shortages, drought, and illness. The results revealed higher stress levels during the dry season and in relation to the measures taken by farmers in protecting their fields. Measurements of the recovery phase are more complicated, as the response depends on wide variations in experiences, genetics, and environments. The effects of coping in cases of reality will differ from coping in cases of presumed or exaggerated stress.

Stress may also be measured by levels of substance P, encephalin, endomorphin -2, mu opioid receptor (mor) and neurokinin-1 receptor expression. The Stress response is dependent on many factors including stressor type, intensity, frequency and duration, characteristics and health status of the individual under stress, and framed cause.

In the chronic stress state, inflammation levels are increased, mental and physical functions are decreased, and long term diseases are more likely to be prevalent. The routine measurement of stress levels should be considered for conditions like obesity, diabetes, heart disease, cancer, dementias, neurodegenerative diseases, autoimmune diseases and glaucoma.

CHAPTER TWO
CAUSES OF STRESS

Key Words: stressor, environmental, physical extremes, exposure to chemical and biological toxins, pathogens, catastrophic events, urban crowding, noise pollution, nutritional deficiencies, social relationships, financial and social status, poverty, racism, emotional, acute and chronic illness, high stress jobs, homelessness, loneliness, fear, perceived threat, eustress, distress, lack of transportation or communication

"Poverty entails fear and stress and sometimes depression. It meets with a thousand petty humiliations and hardships."

J.K. ROWLING

"Much of the stress that people feel doesn't come from having too much to do. It comes from not finishing what they've started."

DAVID ALLEN

"Fear in the mind causes stress in the body."

MARC DRISCOLL

"Stress, anxiety, and depression are caused when we are living to please others."
PAULO COELHO

"Reality is the leading cause of stress among those in touch with it."
LILY TOMLIN

A stressor is any activity, stimulus or event that causes imbalance of mind, body & spirit that may or may not lead to the disruption of harmony. Stressors in the external environment elicit internal responses. Different stressors generate different patterns of the Sympathetic Nervous System (SNS) and hypothalamus-pituitary-adrenal axis (HPA) responses. A healthy system will respond differently than an unhealthy one. Acute stressors result in healthy consequences providing there is recovery and chronic stressors result in adverse consequences depending on conditions of the stressed recipient.

Stress is a reaction to one's environment, real or imagined. It can have positive or negative ramifications depending on the timing, intensity, duration and nature of the stressor and on the condition of the stressed. Short term acute stress, with the release of hormones designed to activate fight or flight muscles and nerves, is normal and healthy as long as recovery is complete. Long term chronic stress is abnormal, destructive, damaging, and the causes may be environmental and/or emotional. Better associated with the response of worrying, the list of causes/stressors, is long. Though both stress reactions are universal in all living organisms, certain stress responses are specific for and most commonly found in certain societies and environments.

American Psychological Association's Top Causes of Chronic Stress

1. Job pressure:(colleague rivalry, deadlines, absence of support, unemployment, job insecurity)
2. Finances: (acute loss, retirement, anticipation of loss, medical expenses, not enough to cover basic expenses, unpaid bills, new bills, missed deadlines) *MoneyInequality*
3. Education: (inadequate access, completion and /or application*) Status*
4. Health: (inadequate access, crisis, terminal illness, $ to pay for Rx, anticipated outcome)
5. Relationships: (arguments, isolation, loneliness, emotional and physical abuses) *Family, Friends*
6. Poor nutrition: (inadequate quality, processed & refined food intake, toxins) *Health*
7. Media overload: (overexposure to shock and alarm and disaster news)
8. Sleep deprivation: (poor quality, low quantity)
9. Daily annoyances: car trouble, clutter, family misbehavior, snubs, insults, discrimination based on skin color, ethnicity, gender, age, sexual orientation, us vs them remarks or attitude, dehumanization) *Racism Privilege*
10. Negative life events: (divorce, conflict, death, disaster loss, fires, storms, floods, temperature extremes, wars, failures, rejections)
11. Loss of independence: (ageing, loss of control, degenerated family relationships, home, work, feeling unwanted and useless *Loneliness / Caregiving*
12. Individual response: the stressor in itself may be stressful and cause more stress hormone release, especially if

it is negative leading to more anxiety, more worry and higher fear response resulting in still more stress.

Most stressors are a combination of environmental and social situations and elicit a similar combination of physical and emotional responses.

Common Causes of Stress

One of the main causes of chronic stress in "modern" societies is Inequality. The rich suffer from the anxiety of maintaining their wealth, while the poor suffer from depression and lack of resources needed to acquire and maintain self-esteem and a means of living. Racism and poverty provide a lifetime of stress from daily insults to profound effects on socioeconomic status. And worse since it is based on a contrived concept without scientific basis and is well known in intellectual circles but allowed to perpetuate through complete ignorance. Finances or lack of, involving debts, responsibilities, threats, and demands can lead to high levels of chronic stress with all organs affected and usually undesirable outcomes. Loneliness, besides its association with poor health, is being recognized as a major cause of drug use, addiction and possible death.

Environmental Causes of Stress

Physical stress can be associated with location, be it of extreme cold, heat, wet or dry, as in highlands, desert, tropics, or jungle. All can take a toll on the human body leaving it with reduced immunity and susceptible to specific diseases. City life can expose one to overcrowding, crime, pollution sites, noise, electromagnetic fields, chemical and biological toxins, toxic food, drug access and addictions, lack of adequate preventive health care, inadequate living conditions, and lack of effective exercise. Rural life, despite the beauty of natural surroundings and health benefit of clean air, can expose one to isolation and lack of access to amenities.

Vignette #3: *A new factory opens in a rural community of 2000 inhabitants. Employing 300 locals and 400 from main town and surrounding countryside, it manufactures plastic tubing for medical facilities. Over a relatively short period of time, cancer rates soar, as well as rates of heart disease and diabetes. Is there an association? What caused this? Stress, both physical in the exposure to toxins, change of diet from rural to urban, more capital to purchase modern goods, fast food, electronics, more sedentary lifestyle... using cars, walking less, changes in hierarchy, women with more responsibilities, competition, and more exposure to toxic substances.*

Catastrophic events like natural disasters and man-made events (war), can lead to traumatic shock (such as post hurricane disaster and PTSD) and bad news, such as a huge IRS or medical bill, can elicit physical and emotional response. The fact that in many cases, help is inadequate serves to compound the stress by prolonging its chronicity and raising its intensity.

Inadequate living conditions and inconvenient location can involve overexposure to toxins, such as housing developments near known nuclear waste sites. Long commute for menial jobs, no access to fresh nutritious food, lack of decent education facilities, receiving daily racial slurs. Daily encounters with aggression be it from peers or police are all causes of stress associated with "modern" living as characterized by industrialization for basic needs, mega-agriculture for food supply and dependency on pharmaceuticals for health maintenance. A day does not pass without receiving scornful looks, murmured insults, grudging service, denial of entry, hesitations, unwelcome attitude, lack of genuine acceptance, constant reminders of low status and fear of failure. Exposure to deep-seated hatred can lead to feelings of uneasiness, dread and non-productivity that are all part of the chronic stress syndrome.

Table 1. TOP INFLAMMATION CAUSING FOODS

Alcohol	Refined white sugar
Refines white flour (with gluten)	Processed meats
Dairy products	Red meats
Canned foods	Trans fats, hydrogenated vegetable oils

Table 2. TOP ANXIETY CAUSING FOODS

1. Tofu/Soy is a lean protein which can disrupt hormonal balance and metabolism
2. Coffee and caffeinated drinks block the uptake of Vitamins D and B, which are needed to balance mood
3. Processed foods contain BPA, which can alter genes in the brain needed to control stress
4. Fructose sugars (HFCS) change the way the brain handles stress, may lead to extreme "bouncing off the wall" anxiety
5. Sugar, caffeine, alcohol, starches, and white bread are foods that trigger stress anxiety
6. Nicotine stimulates the body reacts to increase the production of bad cortisol. It might SEEM like it is reducing stress but is actually contributing to it biochemically.

Poverty is a direct cause of stress. Never having enough, the stress of overwhelming debt, illness is compounded by payments due for medical treatment, lack of community support (safety net), decline of jobs, inequality fueling decline in physical and mental health, daily insult of being inferior in quality, or never being "good enough". Lack of basic nutritional needs lead directly to stress. Low natural omega 3 and omega 6, fatty acid and antioxidants intake can lead to reduced iron uptake, iron deficiency anemia, malnutrition, weakness, impaired cognition, and metabolic dysfunction.

The "drug culture" includes both legal and illegal drugs and is a major source of both acute and chronic stress. Modern society's reliance on painkillers, both over the counter (OTC) and prescribed, is well documented. In addition to direct effects, the stress of acquisition, withdrawal and over-medication is ever present.

Vignette #4: *Medications stress: At a routine clinic visit, an 82 year old patient is found to be taking 17 medications for HBP, arthritis, diabetes, cardiovascular, GU, GI... Glyburide, Irbesartan, Gabapentin, Multivitamin (generic), KCl, Simethicone, Centrum Silver, Vit B12, Simvastatin, a stool softener, Tamsulosin, Phenytoin, Levothyroxine, Sulfacetamide Sodium, Ecodolac, Furosemide, and Aspirin. All systems are affected and side effects from each are being countered by another. His C-reactive protein inflammation index is off the chart (CRP = 45, normal is 1 – 3 mg/L).*

Social and Emotional Causes of Stress

A major source of Stress is "other" people. The actions and interactions of fellow humans have been stressors from before

Homo sapiens became sapient. All animals exhibit responses to presence and activity of family, friends, rivals, and enemies. The majority of stressors that elicit and emotional response are socioeconomic or purely social. In some cases anxiety and stress may occur in the absence of an identifiable cause in such a way as to be more purely of emotional origin.

Financial status in arrears can be a source of incredible stress dealt upon an individual or group, due to debts on a home or incurred by medical bills (in the USA, the cost may be go up to $600,000 for diagnosis and one month treatment of an infection). Such stress creates and compounds the illness and is the #1 cause of foreclosures in USA. Surprise bills, no under insurance and the lack of access to health care, are very common and sometimes catastrophic sources of both acute and chronic stress. For people of privilege, who expect to be at the top and are not, or have a lot but want more, the feeling of falling behind and not attaining wealth fast enough, or not seeing the prospect of attaining wealth as what is expected by society, is a source of chronic stress. When the solution is to accept the frustration of failure, one may turn to drugs, alcoholism, suicide, depression, and anxiety, and become susceptible to *diseases of despair*, to be discussed in the next chapter. For those at or near the bottom rungs of the ladder, chronic stress exists on a daily basis, as associated with inadequate living conditions, poor nutrition, lack of access to health care of any kind, poor education, and absence of a positive mind-uplifting existence.

Work related stressors exist in the form of colleague rivalries and jealousies, effects of your own performance, demands, and your own expectations against results. Any change of venue, loss of job, taking on a new job, retirement, loss of independence, loss of "importance", interpreted as loss of value, goes into the chronic stress column.

With the emotional issues that accompany low self-esteem, the mind and thought processes are affected and influence relationships at home, work, school, finances, nutrition and physical health. Social stressors, such as physical threats, negative comments based on appearance and status, and other ills, contribute to a waste of valuable energy just to get to the field so that the energy needed for playing the field is used up. Images of threat and fear, emotions of anger and resentment and loss of mental fitness lead to loss of rest, sleep and lack of vital rejuvenation are routine factors in chronic stress. Suppression of anger, frustration, grief and guilt become daily factors in the production of stress based on intrinsic fear of failure. Further, a society separated by skin color, the "us vs them" system, separation in schools, absence of interaction between groups, allows for pervasive stress which may erupt into an explosion whenever the two do meet. Intrinsic pressures can be derived from "overthinking" in the form of worry, insomnia, obsession with a problem, questions and doubts for solutions, overanalyzing, expecting the worst or having someone else decide for you. Being overly critical, placing blames elsewhere, and repeatedly regretful, all contribute to perpetual tension and chronic stress.

Family and personal relationships, child-bearing and rearing, teenage problems, and caring for elderly or disabled family member are all major sources of stress, whether accompanied by guilt, physical and emotional attachment or detachment. Change and upheaval through marriage issues, domestic abuse, divorce, or family death leading to disruption of routine, all contribute to chronic stress. Toxic communications at work, at home, in the neighborhood lead to heated arguments or quiet stewing, can lead to anger and distress.

Loneliness or a low level of social interaction and lack of support of any kind, is a prominent stress factor, having a high cause-effect connection to inflammation, and leads directly to high cortisol and epinephrine release in the form of chronic stress. When occurring in early life, the association with heart disease and reduced immunity are especially apparent. In the short term, both homesickness (cortisol release) and lovesickness (dopamine and oxytocin release) exhibit similar symptoms of chronic stress. Loneliness is associated with drug use and alcohol and opioid addiction, ill health equivalent to smoking 15 cigarettes a day and increased risk of death by 30%. Likewise, these factors have a direct effect on heart function, the immune system, adrenal hormone release, and basal metabolism, all contributing to poor health. In addition, isolation often leads to feelings of emotional doom.

Vignette #5: *For a fictional Jules Le Malchanceux, the stress of loneliness in the midst of financial uncertainty, mired in a less than desirable job, confined to less than adequate living conditions, and subjected to a sudden blast by an unexpected bill results in a deep feeling of drowning, nausea of bad feeling and depths of despair, with a profound lack of drive to combat it and at a loss for any kind of solution, the only option is depression.*

Real and perceived threats can lead to fear of bodily harm and trigger the release of adrenalin in the "fight or flight or freeze" system, which developed as a survival mechanism. Failure to recognize the threat and manage it properly, can lead to inappropriate responses (fight a bear but run from a small dog) and recurrent chronic stress. Threats can be verbal or implied, such as with workplace and interfamilial jealousies, rivalries and unfair competition.

Sudden or prolonged illness, whether terminal or temporary, is a source of stress. Health challenging events like brain ageing, neurological disease, cancer, child death, accidental and expected family death are all stressful events. Conflicts between the way things are and the way they are supposed to be, weighs heavily on one's beliefs, values, goals and reality. These are intrinsic factors that lead to extrinsic manifestations of stress.

Marriage, job promotion, baby arrival, and winning the lottery can all be stressful, as in Eustress. Meanwhile, divorce, job loss, demotion, public and private humiliation, abuse, injury and loss of finances, friends or family will trigger Distress.

BOTH Environmental and Social

Vignette #6: *On a Caribbean Island with pristine beaches, rolling hills, sustainable agriculture and a local population known for its longevity, the introduction of tourism and subsequent influx of a urbanites, modernity, land purchases with erection of fences and private signs, segregation, supermarket food, cars replacing donkey carts, lead to a drastic reduction in longevity. Centenarians were reduced to octogenarians and the incidences of cancer, hypertension, heart disease and* diabetes *were significantly increased.*

Due to a combination of stress, both physical and emotional, in the way of supermarket artificial food and loss of control of the land to outsiders, who ignore and/or exploit them, the population lost its handle on stress and succumbed to the frailties and diseases of modern life.

Bullying has long been a factor in the generation of stress both for the perpetrator and the victim. In the USA it is currently a health problem as a cause of chronic and sustained stress, both physical and emotional. Bullies seek status and power over "others" that they consider weaker than themselves, when in effect, they are the weaker set. The damage done in terms of image, performance and productivity, to the one being bullied is probably on the same level as that of alcohol and drugs.

Environmental, Economic, and Social Causes

Homelessness is one of the strongest causes of chronic debilitating stress. In 2017, 553,742 people or 17 of every 17,000 in the USA were homeless. The homeless die 30 years earlier than the general population, due to a combination of poor health and severe depression. The lack of empathy and compassion of the general population toward the homeless in a nation of great wealth is astounding and serves to add to the deep stress caused by the situation. Being unwanted, uncared for, and deemed a failure is the deepest form of chronic physical and emotional stress imaginable.

Vignette #7: *There is a high level of chronic stress in some 800,000 Deferred Action for Childhood Arrivals (DACA) immigrant children living with the fear and threat of being rounded up and sent back to a country with which they have no connection. Some 63% of Dreamers exhibited psychological distress (loss of home, social status, and family, marginalization, discrimination, isolation, no option for travel abroad and limited opportunities), harsh living conditions, and lack of access to mental health services, which constitute both mental and environmental health hazards as referenced in a study by Luz Garcini at Rice University, Texas.*

Not belonging and existing in limbo lead to fear and anxiety which result in poor performance and low achievement which serve to confirm the negative expectations that were present in the first place. In the meantime, stress is compounded by a Congress, apparently too mean to enact the DREAM Act, or by the desires of their constituents, who are too mean to care.

Jenny Tung at the Duke University Institute for Brain Sciences and Luis Barreiro at the University of Montreal in a study on the analysis of immune cells and gene expression of female macaques before and after they artificially changed the relative social status of the animals (by creating new social groups), that a lower social status directly affected the immune system as linked to higher levels of inflammation and a change in the animals' immune cell make up. Similar physical and emotional changes may affect the disadvantaged in the lower levels of human society.

Social racism is intricately linked to both acute and chronic stress. countries where people are separated into "different races" based on skin color, which is biologically incorrect, intrinsic fear and hatred produce extrinsic threats, poor communications, separate cuisines, facilities, schools, housing, churches and work places, despite living together in the same country for centuries, the environmental and emotional stress is constant and pervasive. These countries will never achieve full health and contentment as long as tis level of stress persists.

Vignette #8: *In 1996, after 20 years as an ophthalmic surgeon, and upon presenting myself wearing a suit to the head of the operating theater at a prominent hospital in Atlanta, Georgia, I was shown the closet with the mop and broom... as, no doubt, the newly hired janitor.*

Armed with this experience, I fully understood the insults to Barack Obama's throughout the 8 years of his presidency, from the birther nonsense which was tolerated by the news media and the entire US population, the beer with the campus officer in Massachusetts, to the congressional refusal to consider his nominee for the Supreme Court, and to vote for a single one of his proposals, are all examples of chronic stress. A mean look, refusal to smile and greet a fellow rider in an elevator or upon entering a store or restaurant, dispenses chronic stress. The daily added burdens imposed on people of color in the USA when carrying out mundane routine chores and tasks, is chronic stress. School assignments, choices, social pairings or lack of are demonstrated in the fact that people of color (POC) and white people do not speak to each other. Having completely different accents while living in the same space is a result of the chronic stress of separation. Fear and hatred of "Mexicans and Muslims", desires to expel and shut out "others", dating back to the frontier mentality of fears from threats of savage Native American raids, are examples of chronic stress. Fear of losing money, and hence position and power and privilege, lead to the election of a dangerous individual who promised to take away the chronic stress of some and impose it on others.

Table 3. OCCUPATIONAL STRESS

Low Stress Jobs:	High Stress Jobs:
Lawyer	Doctor/ Nurse
Garbage collector	Lawyer with a conscience
Burger flipper	Teacher
Clergy	Restauranteur
Farmer with fertilizers and pesticides	Farmer with organics only
Ticket collector	Military front line
IRS agent	Airline Pilot
Car mechanic	Race car driver

Occupation has a great impact on stress levels of doctors and nurses, where the job demands a stronger, more sustained stress response, continuation and repetition, and higher chance of reduced recovery experience, rendering these individuals to higher risks of poorer mental and physical health.

Stressors are universal in the human experience. How one responds and the methods used for management determine the outcomes. In the chronic stress state, inflammation levels are increased, mental and physical functions are decreased, and long term diseases are more likely to be prevalent.

CHAPTER THREE
STRESS AND DISEASE

Key words: acute stress, immune system, cytokines, regulatory and killer T cells, phagocytosis, organ systems, inflammation, autoimmune, medical illness, psychiatric illness, cancer, cardiovascular system, central nervous system, digestion, diabetes, urinary tract, respiratory disorders, toxic patient

"It's not stress that kills us, it is our reaction to it."

HANS SELYE

"The less you respond to rude, critical, argumentative people, the more peaceful your life will become..."

CHARLES M. SCHULZ

"I believe that stress is a factor in any bad health."

CHRISTOPHER SHAYS

"A sad soul can kill you quicker, far quicker, than a germ."

JOHN STEINBECK

"Inflammation is the body's reaction to stress."

DAN BUETTNER

"In times of life crisis...the first thing I do is go back to basics...am I eating right, am I getting enough sleep, am I getting some physical and mental exercise every day."

EDWARD ALBERT

"Nothing is worth your Health. Nothing is worth poisoning yourself into Stress, anxiety and fear."

STEVE MARABOLI

"Plants exhibit responsive behavior to stressors! Stressed plants get sick and sometimes die. The most important requirement for a successful stress response is to be in good health. To be in poor health and subjected to stressors, will just make matters worse."

ALFRED L ANDUZE

Inflammation is the root cause usually associated with almost every disease or condition that afflicts human beings... cancer, heart disease, stroke, dementias, diabetes, gastric disorders, neurological and autoimmune disease. Stress is a major cause of inflammation. A chronic repeated physiological reaction it elicits can lead to damage to all organ systems. The effects of stress on the mind and body play much more of a role in disease processes than modern medicine accounts for and addresses. More time, energy and resources are devoted to treating the symptoms than in addressing the causes. If we paid more attention to the interplay of stress and disease, we would be a much healthier people.

STRESS AND INFLAMMATION = DISEASE

History of Stress and Disease

In ancient Greek medicine, the qualities of the four humors were thought to be the causes of all diseases. Yellow bile caused warm diseases like liver cirrhosis and was associated with emotional anger. Phlegm caused cold diseases of the lungs and respiratory apparatus, and black bile was associated with melancholy and depression. Blood disorders caused sluggishness and infections. In addition, chronic repetitive fear was associated with cardiovascular diseases and apathy with stomach diseases. Emotions and diseases were very closely related.

Statistics for Stress and Disease

The top ten leading causes of death in USA are stress-related: coronary heart disease, cancer, respiratory disorders, accidental injuries, influenza-pneumonia infections, stroke, diabetes, kidney disease, cirrhosis of the liver, Alzheimer's, and suicide.

1. 75 to 90% of all doctor visits are for stress-related diseases
2. 43% of all adults suffer adverse health effects from stress
3. Lifetime prevalence of emotional disorder = 50%
4. 40% of deaths are from stress-related disease (CVD, stroke & especially cancer)
5. Metabolic Syndrome (hypertension, diabetes, cardiovascular deficiencies, Obesity, high triglycerides, high cholesterol) carries a high risk for a poor outcome, as all are associated with high inflammation indices and high chronic stress levels.
6. 293 independent studies done between 1960 and 2001, confirm that stress alters immunity. Stressed immune

cells, as in viral colds, are less sensitive to hormones that turn off inflammation, therefore, inflammation continues.

7. USA suicide rate is highest in 30 years, with a 2.3% increase
8. Accidents are up to 6.7%, some linked to social and financial stressors, and opioid addictions with 28,000 killed in 2014, plus car crashes, falls, and suffocation
9. Heart disease is up by 1% and stroke up by 3%, related to hypertension, poor diet and lack of exercise
10. Alzheimer's dementia up by 15.7%, toxins, poor diet and large number of elderly
11. Diabetes with a 1.9% increase, due to diet (obesity) and lack of exercise
12. Kidney up 1.5% and Respiratory disease up 2.7%, with decreased immunity
13. Cancer rate decreased by 1.7%, associated with earlier detection and improved treatment.

Vignette #9: *The Russian leader, Vladimir Lenin, died of "constant rage", according to his wife, Nadezhda Krupskaya, directed at trying and failing to initiate a viable economic process for the Soviet Union 1918 to 1924. His death was attributed to complications from the process of acute and chronic stress.*

Physiological Signs and Symptoms of Stress

Sympathetic secretions of cortisol and epinephrine lead to bad feeling, nausea, fear, empty hollow feeling, such as with homesickness, lovesickness, nervousness before a performance, a speech, or a leap from a high place. When repeated even if at various intensities, these may lead to metabolic dysfunction and disease, as well as worsening of existing diseases.

Acute responses include an increased heart rate, increased respiration, headache, stiff neck, tight shoulders, back pain, sweaty palms, and upset stomach with nausea, vomiting or diarrhea. Your response here depends highly on body health: how intense the stressor, its duration, and what kind of condition your coping mechanisms are in. If there is heart disease with an abnormal circulation or a dysfunctional central nervous system, then arrhythmias, heart attack or stroke may occur. If the body and mind are in good condition, then a good, sharp, hormonal reaction has a protective purpose that leads to recovery and keeps the immune system in tune. The release of acute inflammation cytokines will give off mostly heat, redness, and swelling of the skin, for purposes of repair. With an extreme acute reaction to stress that leads to a panic attack, there is a sudden intense fear or anxiety, with shortness of breath, dizziness, heart pounding seemingly out of control, and a weak feeling "like dying". In the acute response, recovery is the usual rule.

Vignette #10: *JM, a 76 year old lady suffered an acute anxiety attack while sitting in the waiting area being prepped for a fluorescein angiography procedure of the eyes for routine follow up of the status of her diabetic retinopathy. The anticipation of pain and discomfort of the fluid dye injection coupled with living with high levels of stress for a very long time "was just too much for me!" The procedure was rescheduled and done without incident the following week.*

Vignette #11: *My Blood Pressure averages 120/80 up from 120/72 since I entered my sixties and reduced the athletic distance running and weekly sports regimen. In anticipation of a hurricane with its destruction of property and inconveniences of*

41

life in aftermath, my BP shot up to 180/110, at risk for heart disease range. In absence of demonstrative cardiovascular pathology and in the calm after the storm, it returned to a comfortable 130/82. Such are the effects of "stress", physical and emotional.

Chronic responses engage the inflammation pathway at a different level. In unmanaged stress, the acute responses may be present but due to longer duration, at a lower intensity, so that the body and mind can tolerate it for longer periods of time without shutting down. At the physiological level, blood sugar levels increase, giving insulin insensitivity, which may lead to diabetes. Sugar cravings (as the hormone leptin is released) lead to higher food intake, usually in the form of carbohydrates and fats, all leading to weight gain and obesity. The resulting INFLAMMATION can lead to an acceleration of ageing, general pain and many disease conditions.

Vignette #12: *Concerning Chronic Open Angle Glaucoma: In 1976, my introduction to glaucoma as a resident, consisted of measuring serial eye pressures with a handheld Schiotz tonometer on patients over several 24 hour periods, as art of Dr. John C. Merritt's ground breaking cannabis with the THC at the delta 9 position study in the attempt to lower the eye pressures in cases of advanced glaucoma. Several hundred patients later, revealed that the eye pressures were indeed lowered substantially with cannabis inhalation, but the side effects, mode of delivery and frequency precluded routine use. Despite treatment, many progressed to end-stage blindness as continues to occur today despite more advanced technology. Upon examination of advanced progressive cases, one will find that the majority are associated with high levels of stress... i.e. young black males, older black males and females, under stress of physical environment and daily emotional insults. No one had a "stress-free life". With morbidity and response to medication listed as "worse" in blacks. The same "blacks" have much higher levels of stress than other groups. In a high percentage of Black American males subjected to prison life, ghetto glaucoma, hypertension, diabetes, poor nutrition, and toxin exposure, all have high levels of stress. I suggest that physicians pay more attention to stress levels when diagnosing and formulating treatment regimens for your patients.*

Diseases Associated with Stress: Effects on Organ Systems

Table 4. STRESS-RELATED DISEASES

Lupus erythematosus	Allergies	Asthma
Cancers: breast, prostate, colon	Multiple myeloma	Thyroid diseases
Digestive problems	Infections: HIV, colds, herpes	Diabetes
Rheumatoid arthritis	Heart disease: hypertension	Vasculitis
Headaches: tension, migraine	Skin disorders	Depression & anxiety, autism
Alzheimer's: dementias	Multiple sclerosis	Obesity
Lung: COPD, emphysema	Liver disease: hepatitis, cirrhosis	Premature ageing
Kidney: cystic fibrosis, nephritis	Eye: macular degen, glaucoma	Chronic fatigue syndrome

Immune System: The prototype of an immune system disease directly associated with stress is Lupus erythematosus, in which "normal" cells attack their own tissue. The incidence is high in women, 20-40 year age group, and African American, Latinos and Asian minority groups. These are the same groups with high levels of stress, which range from environmental causes, living next to toxic dumps, oil and gas facilities, in low income housing, drug use and side effects and from emotional causes. There may be joint pain, "butterfly" shaped skin rash on the face, neck and hands, sensitivity to ultraviolet sunlight to the skin and eyes, patchy hair loss, abnormal high protein levels in the kidneys, inflammation of the external layers of the heart (pericarditis), and difficulty breathing from inflammation in the lungs.

Chronic repeated stress disrupts and destroys the immune system. The production of macrophage and T-cells that normally respond to acute inflammation and prevent cancers is inhibited by the high level of cortisol produced by chronic stress. Constant worry leads to adrenal fatigue which results in anxiety, depression, sleep disorders with reduced chances of recovery, heart disease and digestive issues.

Chronic exposure to formaldehyde is connected to higher incidences of cancer, while exposure to benzene is associated with developmental and neurological defects. High cortisol levels lead to resistance and further improper secondary responses so that the inflammation of arthritis, obesity, fibromyalgia, chronic anxiety and depression are suppressed. If the inflammation continues, the result is a "stressed out", weary, fatigued, confused person with multiple aches and pains, and total dependency on medications for temporary relief. The SICK PERSON has a high inflammation index or C-reactive protein (CRP), high SED rate (red blood cell sedimentation), CBC insufficiency (reduced red and white blood counts), is usually obese, has a poor diet, poor absorption of nutrients due to gastric problems, a constant release of pro-inflammatory cytokines when the body mistakes itself as the enemy and attacks relentlessly, and is susceptible to all manner of organ and system dysfunction. There is a direct relationship between stress, impaired immunity, inflammation, disease and accelerated ageing.

Infections: Exposure to the common cold virus (Rhinovirus) elicits a good group 1 inflammation response directed at containment and mild symptoms. In cases of stress and a weak immune system, elicits a group 2 abnormal inflammation response (high pro-cytokines release) with intense cold symptoms and prolonged duration. The regulation of the inflammation response determines the outcome of the disease.

Brain and Central Nervous System: The excess cortisol released by the HPA axis system in the brain leads directly to inflammation, damage to nerve synapses (connections) in the hypocampus area and a reduction in the control of cortisol feedback, thereby leading to unregulated excess. The immune system in the brain is unable to offer protection to neurons, which succumb to chronic stress as manifested by recurrent headaches, tension in the neck and shoulders, and mental fatigue. A tired brain produced abnormal chemicals which lead to brain shrinkage in the areas that regulate emotions and self-control. Depression & anxiety, dementias, Alzheimer's, Parkinson's, autism, Multiple sclerosis, Amyotrophic lateral sclerosis, migraines, insomnia, bipolar disorders, ADHD, Asperger's syndrome and cancers are some of the conditions associated with chronic stress. In the eyes, macular degeneration, glaucomatous optic neuropathy, cataracts, and retinal degenerations have stress related components. The inflammation response to increased physical stress impairs cognition. In sleep dysfunction associated with stress, high cortisol levels promote wakefulness and the brain is reminded of problems, thereby releasing more cortisol.

> *"In a disordered mind, as in a disordered body,*
> *soundness of health is impossible."*
> CICERO

In the dementias, excess cortisol interferes with the neurotransmitters causing a decreased ability to form new memories through reduced brain cell communications. In Alzheimer's the tangles of neurons and connections are worsened by high levels of cortisol. Some seizures may be triggered by sudden drop in blood pressure associated with acute stress. The symptoms of brain inflammation can be manifested in mood changes, avoidance, brooding, depression and anxiety, edginess, and irritability. The spontaneous recurrence of unpleasant memories and distress upon encountering the decreased memory function are unpleasant hallmarks of Alzheimer's and Parkinson's diseases. With the symptoms of nightmares, flashbacks, forced amnesia, anger, guilt, fear, reduction in creativity, production and decision making, the individual responds with more stress than usual, leading to more cortisol/adrenaline surging and further cognitive decline. Brain shrinkage affects blood pressure regulation and heart health, insulin sensitivity and diabetes, weight regulation and obesity, reduced sexual function leading to generalized negativity and poor health.

Heart and circulation: Inflammation in the blood vessels may lead to hypertension, plaque formation in the coronary arteries, arrhythmias, heart attack and stroke. Symptoms consist of palpitations, increased heart rate, bouts of dizziness and weakness, shortness of breath, and swelling of the lower extremities. A weak immune system along with blood vessel disruption increases the risk of stroke due to narrowing of the arteries and unregulated pressure and volume of flow. Excess epinephrine/adrenalin leads to an increase in blood pressure, an increase in heart rate and a strain on the circulation. Chronic stress may lead to indulgence in comfort foods high in fat and sugar, leading to obesity and more stress, both physical and emotional. Excess cortisol is associated with increased waist fat, which is a direct risk factor for cardiovascular diseases, like hypertension, thromboses, arteriosclerosis, angina, varicose veins, high blood cholesterol, high triglycerides and cancers like multiple myeloma, stroke and myocardial infarction (heart attack). Jobs with high demand and low decision making, family issues, catastrophic daily life events, with high energy output and low self-esteem, lead to an accumulation of damage from hypertension, fatigue and depression, necessitating the call for "need a break". Cardiovascular diseases remain the leading cause of death worldwide and are associated with both chronic emotional and environmental stress.

Lungs: In asthma, both acute and chronic stress amplify the immune response to the triggers, pollen, dust, and dander. When occurring in childhood, it may be associated with adverse emotional events. As smoking may or may not be a coping mechanism for emotional stress, in chronic obstructive pulmonary disease (COPD), the physical damage induced from the action worsens the condition and renders a poorer response to treatment. Bronchitis, emphysema and lung cancer all are associated with immune system deficiency and damage.

Cancer: Chronic stress leads to a weakened immune system, which allows for the uncontrolled growth of abnormal cells that use up nutrients and eventually, space. Excess stress hormones activate the inflammation response in damage mode, which causes the immune system repair mechanism to form abnormal cells whose programmed cell death (apoptosis) is blocked, leading to the formation of more abnormal cells, as well as a reduction in natural killer cells, inhibition of DNA repair, stimulation of new blood vessel formation (angiogenesis) which feeds more cancers cells and the activation of "epithelial- mesenchymal transition" which also creates new cancer stem cells. In addition to the physical stress, there is also an emotional component which leads to further immune system suppression and concomitant cancer cell proliferation. In breast cancer progression and outcomes, there is a direct correlation of risk and incidence with stressful events, life changing events like death, personal illness, divorce, and loss of livelihood. In prostate cancer, men with high stress levels and lack of satisfying relationships are at 3X higher risk than men in stable relationships with low stress levels. There is a close link between emotional stress and cancer development, progression or regression. Strong supportive treatment with emphasis on stress management is mandatory in all cases of cancer.

Diabetes: In chronic stress, the liver produces and adds glucose to the blood stream as fuel for required energy. When this occurs repeatedly, excess glucose is dumped into the tissues, leading to weight gain and eventual obesity. Obesity, closely linked to inflammation, induces the abnormal release of insulin from pancreas, which raises insulin resistance and leads to diabetes. In black obese women, the association with diabetes is disproportional. Some blood sugar increases are stress-related not only from food intake, but in the recall of stressful life situations, leads to epinephrine release and spikes in blood sugar. Diabetes as an increase insulin resistance and a decrease in insulin sensitivity is linked to a majority of major diseases, like heart disease, hypertension, cancer, digestive system issues, inflammatory diseases, and neurological degenerations.

Digestive System: Leaky gut, Irritable Bowel Syndrome, Ulcerative colitis, Gastroesophageal Reflux Disease (GERD) and hepatitis are all stress-related. High cortisol and epinephrine trigger the release of excess histamines which change the concentration of hydrochloric acid in the stomach, which produces indigestion (reduced absorption of nutrients) and inflammation, resulting in various degrees of gastritis, enteritis, colitis, peptic ulcers, constipation, and diarrhea. The immune system is weakened when blood factors are released that attack the digestive system at its weakest (inflammation) points and when the person uses coping mechanisms of alcohol and/or compensatory overeating.

Kidneys and Bladder: Chronic stress from toxin accumulation of foods, drugs, and pollutants, can lead to infection and inflammation (nephritis and cystitis), as well as high blood pressure, fluctuations in blood vessel walls and blood flow dynamics. These organs act as filters for the entire circulation. Early symptoms of stress may manifest as lower back pain and frequent urination. Stress and anxiety may lead to an overactive bladder as an over stimulated muscle pushes urine out. This is a natural part of the "fight or flight" reaction, and worrying about it can compound the situation. Repetitive intense coughing, toxic smoking and obesity can also contribute to stress incontinence.

Muscles and Bones: Muscles can contract as much as 5% during intense activities, but bone can be strained only about 0.5% before it begins to fail, hence leading to a small crack or "stress fracture". Both must rest in order to recover and rebuild.

Chronic physical and emotional stress (high cortisol levels) can lead to a weakened immune system that is unable to recover and rebuild, hence inflammation, as manifested in joint pain and reduced mobility. Rheumatoid arthritis and inflammation are classic examples a vicious cycle, as each is a cause of the other and each involves the dissemination of pain. There is a connection of psychological stress with early adverse life events, flare ups and poor responses to treatments. The immune system is very sensitive to an increase in stress hormones, especially catecholamines (norepinephrine and epinephrine) and interferes with the normal regulation of natural killer cells responsible for inflammation control. Osteoarthritis sufferers are more prone to the stresses of old age. In fibromyalgia, a "society disease", the constant tension in muscles of the neck, shoulders, and lower back coupled with the loss of muscle tone, leads to seemingly intractable pain and fatigue. The link with traumatic physical or emotional events and onset of pain has been made to anger and mental stress.

Post-Traumatic Stress Disorder: (PTSD) is usually associated with adverse events in wartime. The intensity and extent of the distress correlates with the scale of the injury and degree of difficulty with the understanding and acceptance of the event. The chronic stress occurs and reoccurs when the victim fails to recover and re-experiences the event as well as accompanying symptoms well after the event has passed. Car accidents, sexual, emotional or physical abuse or assaults, dangerous encounters with animal of vehicle, accidental falls, and substance abuse can also trigger PTSD.

Skin: Stress releases cortisol which interferes with the activities of other hormones that normally regulate skin metabolism. Ageing, wrinkles, acne, rosacea, eczema, fever blisters and psoriasis all are aggravated by stress. Hives and rashes can be the direct result of a stressful event. Emotional stress is the most common trigger for inflammatory skin disorders, which in turn are some of the most common causes of psychological, social and occupational stress. Intensity, severity and duration of symptoms may worsen in the presence of recurrent stress. Physical and psychological stress can lead to an acceleration in biological ageing caused by the shortening of telomeres on the strands of cellular DNA. Constant stress can be the cause of relentless breakdown of the body and mind.

Hair Loss: Premature graying, thinning, and male pattern baldness can be accelerated by chronic stress and the concomitant increase in androgens. There may also be an association with insomnia, depression and anxiety. Hair that thins out due to stress can grow back once the stressors are removed or controlled.

Reproductive System: Both acute and chronic stress inhibit the female reproductive system by activating the HPA axis system in the brain to reduce estrogens and progesterone and shut down function, leading to low fertility, pregnancy problems, premenstrual syndrome (PMS), amenorrhea, and dysmenorrhea. Reduce sex drive (libido) occurs in both male and female. Stress can affect the male system in erectile dysfunction, impotence, reduced testosterone levels, and reduced sperm count and quality. Sex appeal is diminished as there is often decreased attraction to ne who is "stressed out".

Genetic defects& diseases can be triggered by chronic stress as it stimulates the release or inhibition of growth hormone production (via cytokine release), leading to decreases in Growth hormone sensitivity, binding protein, expression of growth hormone receptors and liver sensitivity to growth hormone.

Production and expressions of many enzymes vital to basic metabolism, such as blood production and flow, sugar levels, nutrient absorption, muscle function, digestion, inflammation and elimination are all dependent on levels and instructions of hormones.

Oxidative Stress as a Cause of Disease

In all the organ systems mentioned, psychological and physical stress are manifested at the chemical and cellular levels through the process of oxidative stress, or breakdown of cells and tissues from free radicals in the form of oxygen and reactive oxygen species. The effects may be good, as reactive oxygen species (ROS) can be beneficial when the immune system uses oxygen to attack and disable pathogens. Cells may then respond by increasing good hormones and eliminate toxins thereby reducing ageing. Under adverse conditions with chronic stress and abnormal amounts of disruptive hormones, most oxidative stress processes (ROS) appear to have damaging effects.

Event Stressors are typically associated with cardiovascular disease, hypertension, arrhythmias, heart attack, stroke, Digestive disorders, stomach ulcers, gastritis, enteritis and Cancers. Emotional stressors (anger, aggravation, agitation) are typically associated with rheumatoid arthritis, skin problems, migraine, digestive problems, strong and prolonged negative emotions, chronic fatigue syndrome, and a reduction in protective immune defenses, autoimmune and neurological diseases. Considerable overlap and combinations are the rule.

Emotional Effects of Stress

"Diseases of the soul are more dangerous and more numerous than those of the body."

CICERO

"To avoid sickness, eat less; to prolong life, worry less."

CHU HUI WENG

Depression and anxiety may be diseases of the body, but are closely related to levels of stress present. Disease feeds off stress and peaks and valleys depend on the status of the mind and body. Stress causes fluctuations in neurotransmitters like dopamine, serotonin and norepinephrine, which leads to mood changes, decreased appetite, impaired sleep and reduced libido. High cortisol levels of long duration may do permanent damage to hippocampus brain cells.

A basic stress response of depression is to shut down physical activity and enter a state of reduced fitness. This lack of exercise leads directly to a decrease in the amount of oxygen available to generate energy for muscles. With reduced muscle strength, tissues grow smaller muscle cells and bigger fat cells, less number of muscle cells and higher number of fat cells, leading to an increased risk of obesity, inflammation, heart disease, hypertension and cancer.

Emotional stress has a direct effect and an indirect effect, both of which are detrimental to health. Smoking as an emotional crutch takes in toxins that cause more physical stress. Emotional stress releases neuropeptides which are protein bits in stress and mood hormones which connect the brain to the body and transmit "feelings" through these neural pathways which give feedback that may do good or harm, such as with love, hate, embarrassment, happiness and sadness. All have an influence on body functions.

The body and mind may react differently to the same situation. Stress anxiety or depression is the physical and emotional reaction to threat or challenge and can be different in different individuals depending on their history, environment, status, situation, and mental status. An upcoming wedding party may evoke happy feelings in one planner and dire feelings in another. Driving in rush hour may give rise to extreme anger in one and relaxation or welcome boredom in another. A regular anxiety reaction to challenges is generally associated with heart disease, depression and cancers.

How stress affects the way you think, act and feel, coupled with daily deficiencies in diet, shelter, basic needs; a deficiency of joy, being unable to appreciate the little things; subjected to daily insults and humiliations no matter how seemingly small that accumulate and leave marks; restlessness, constant fear, malaise being unproductive, uncreative, inefficient; irritability, apathy, covetous of desires for things out of reach, all and each are capable of creating and worsening many medical conditions. Poor decisions, endless and insurmountable difficulties serve to activate and promote long term stress levels, more cortisol release, more inflammation and more disease. When one responds to stress by entering the realm of drug relief, isolation and severe anger, emotional stress is compounded and becomes deep-seated and seemingly immobile.

Vignette #13: *The emotional stress level of my brother, as a result of the loss of his son, Gregory, my nephew, and of not having been able to have done anything to save him from the ravages of liver disease, was so severe that he could no longer entertain and play the music he loved. His frustration and anger developed into dysfunction and disability, compounded by increased intake of legal toxins in cigarettes, drowning in alcohol and greatly reduced nutrition, until his body broke down. The physical stress of the pain and agony in the body was compounded by the financial burden of the cost of treatment. His date with death had been signed and sealed from the onset of the disease.*

Fear: Activates the area in the brain known as the amygdala. The area lights up when a person sees the face of an intruder or "other" person deemed as a threat. This judgment, made in 1/10 second, in deciding whether to "fight or flight" is made by a low level brain structure, and is based on familiarity, learning, experience and perception. Fear or acceptance determines the level of stress hormone release. Stress-induced changes in brain chemistry by constant reminders of threats (News media) may have permanent damage on the individual psyche.

Loneliness: Is a chronic stress situation with a constantly high cortisol release rate, high blood pressure and high incidence of heart disease, with association in early life. In a study done on healthy college freshmen, it was found that loneliness and a small social network were associated with reduced immunity, and concomitant higher risk of susceptibility to illness due to a low antibody response to flu vaccine. In isolation there is a higher than normal epinephrine release which shuts down viral defenses and inhibits certain protective white blood cells, thereby leading to inflammation of heart, brain, various cancers and arthritis. Loneliness can lead to poor sleep, daytime dysfunction and a rebound stress hormone release in the evenings. Reduced glucose tolerance can lead to type 2 diabetes.

Inequality/Social diseases: Institutional and social racism, discrimination, lack of access to basic living facilities and nutrients, and daily insults all play a role in shaping the personalities, experiences, available coping mechanisms and social support systems of certain groups of people Physical and emotional stress in a modern society leads directly to chronic stress, excess cortisol release and accumulation, inflammation and disease. Hypertension, diabetes, arthritis, glaucoma, prostate cancer, heart disease in women, infections and chronic inflammation are a few of the diseases prominent in the disadvantaged and marginalized groups of the society. Instead of placing blame on "race" and genetics, medicine and society should pay more attention to the role of stress as a cause of disease. The increasing rates of opiate use and suicide at all levels of society can also be traced to increasing levels of stress.

Vignette #14: *Living in Poverty means always jumping up to touch bottom; lacking everything; zero opportunities, limited access; daily stress of living day to day on handouts, hustling; avoiding police, high chance of mass incarceration; males unable to provide, unable to achieve a state of dignity, unable to produce that which is routinely denied them; onset of Stress from birth, high incidence of stress-related disease, hypertension, progressive glaucoma, heart disease, psychological trauma, digestive problems from inadequate nutrition, inadequate access to health care, drug use (responsive and environmental); No sophisticated coping techniques to work with here; no chances of avoidance since most of the stressors are in the environment; very little access to alteration mechanisms; acceptance through religious affiliation and guidance is used as the principal management strategy as is the optional escape with drugs; adaptation with use of music and social strategies are very prevalent. Neglect of facing and dealing with the stress response may lead to death of the mind, spirit and body.*

Vignette #15: *The typical toxic patient comes in for a specific ailment or two and is mostly unaware of the close connection with lifestyle, habits and exposure to toxins. Most are under extreme stress and handle their situations very differently. In examination of the whole patient, many with glaucoma also have hypertension, type 2 diabetes, heart disease, arthritis, cancer, autoimmune condition and any combination. Chronic stress reduces the immune system, promotes an abnormal inflammation response and is associated with the development, progression and poor outcomes of some 80% disease entities.*

The normal human lifespan that is programmed for between 100-120 years is lessened by stress and the reaction to stressors.

CHAPTER FOUR
STRESS MANAGEMENT

Key words: acceptance, adaptation, alteration, avoidance, plan, purpose, sleep quality, social connections, relationships, positive outlook, energy, health, immune system, forgiveness, prayer, faith, grounding, reframing, altruism, breathing exercises, yoga, meditation, laughter, music, color therapy, tai chi, aromatherapy, expressive art therapy, physical activity, exercise, diet and nutrition, cortisol control, adaptogens, drug avoidance, toxins,

"A diamond is a piece of charcoal that handled stress exceptionally well."

UNKNOWN

"Adopting the right attitude can convert a negative stress into a positive one... It is how you react to the stressor that determines the outcome. It is your choice."

HANS SELYE

"Stress should be a driving force not an obstacle."

BILL PHILLIPS

> *"When we commit to action, to actually doing something rather than feeling trapped by events, the stress in our life becomes manageable."*
>
> GREG ANDERSON

> *"Modern science has yet to produce a tranquilizing medicine as effective as a few kind words."*
>
> SIGMUND FREUD

> *"In life, we lurch from one crisis to another, sometimes solving, more often just coping, but never really entirely free from stress."*
>
> A. L. ANDUZE

Many treatment plans for disease entities involve "diet, exercise, and avoid smoking", but fail to emphasize the effective management of stress. This chapter provides some practical suggestions for tailoring your responses to stressful situations.

Basic Fundamental Rules of Stress Management

In the presence of acute and chronic stress, the main goal for all systems is for a return of the individual to a comfortable state of homeostasis. The first step in stress management is the reduction in frequency, intensity and duration of the cortisol stress response. One should be able to recognize both acute and chronic stress, know the feeling, recognize the source, and summon effective responses to offset the destructive effects of stress hormones. By understanding and addressing the nature of the stressor, the individual can use the basic reaction and choose the best techniques to control the result. The secondary response goal is the prevention of abnormal inflammation. The most crucial factor in the stress response is the health status of the individual. In the average individual, basic good health with a functional immune system and adequate energy stores is required for handling a normal inflammation response and preventing an abnormal one. In chronically stressed individuals, strong effective coping mechanisms are required to achieve a disease free state.

Table 5. GOOD HEALTH: KEEP THE IMMUNE SYSTEM FUNCTIONAL

Positive attitude	Stress control, relaxation	Regular exercise
Healthy nutrition	Social interactions	Toxins avoidance

In a stressful situation where the response heavily influences the result, first recognize the presence of a stressor, then decide on a plan of action. Coping strategies can be presented in four categories, acceptance, adaptation, alteration and avoidance, and several combinations of each. With responses that take the form of acceptance, like ignore and forgive, the "don't let it bother me" attitude, the release of cortisol may or may not be contained. With responses like adaptation or alteration, taking the form of reactive eating, food satisfaction linked to brain stress relief, fleeing the scene, or transferring the blame and responsibility to someone or something else, relief may be temporary and the stressor may return stronger than before. Acceptance and adaptation work well in combination. Alteration can be tricky as there may be unwanted side effects. Avoidance appears to be the only foolproof way of handling stress and is also the most difficult to achieve.

Secondly, address the stressor. Do not leave stress unchecked. When you receive the "chemical rush", decide how to formulate a response. Accepting the stressor as it is "it doesn't bother me" or "ignorance is bliss" had better be real. If recognized and suppressed, it accumulates and may be very unhealthy, as in inflammation building. If you accept and submit, as in "Oh poor me", the chronic release moves into the "worry and fret" response, leading to daily damage to both the body and the mind, resulting in emotional anxiety disorders and physical diseases.

Vignette #16: *A wife is the principal caretaker for her husband, who has had a stroke. She does everything for him in addition to working to supplement their income. She does not complain nor seek outside help. In the space of a few years, she develops glaucoma, lupus, depression, HBP, and severe arthritis over a period of a few years. The husband is consumed with his wife's non-existent extramarital affair since his libido and performance are severely compromised. His pathology worsens, and he develops anxiety with panic attacks, depression, severe cardiovascular insufficiency, bronchitis, and enteritis. Neither expresses their deepest concerns.*

> *"I love it when it rains, so no one will see my tears."*
>
> CHARLIE CHAPLIN

When totally unaware of the stressor, is ignorance truly blissful? When truly relaxed or distracted or incapable of recognizing a stressor, such as in Downs Syndrome and cerebral palsy, where genes for stressor recognition and reactive inflammation are probably turned off, it probably is.

From a chemical point of view, effective management strategies for Stress should offset the sympathetic reaction and counteract the excessive release and accumulation of the stress hormones. As a practical function, the individual should react positively and use the best tools at his or her disposal. Keep in mind, mismanagement can and will lead to a worsening of the situation and possible disease scenarios.

Accepting the Inevitable: Positive Outlook, Faith, Forgiveness, and Prayer

"How do you deal with chronic repetitive stress? You rise above it."

OPRAH WINFREY

Adopting a POSITIVE attitude, you will face the stressor head on and overcome it. After you define your purpose, then you make a plan. Whether it is in response to physical or mental abuse or ostracism, you are choosing to react by facing the problem and overcoming it. You are "taking the bull by the horns", the Minoan principle of bull leaping, and have success as the primary outcome. A positive attitude increases the feel-good chemicals in the brain that promote the immune system. With the glass as half full, and all failures and setbacks as temporary, you set up a base from which to learn, to change and to grow. A positive attitude works well toward recovery from things you cannot change.

To reduce stress levels and maximize the efficiency of the stress response, your personality, mindset, health and expectations must be conducive to positive thinking. A positive outlook can make the brain's gray matter "grow" to accept and deal with the stressful situation. The brain can then process the reactive emotions better so that the response is less intense, less damaging and improves with time. Positive thoughts increase the release of neuropeptides (good proteins) in the brain, boost the immune system functions, reduce blood pressure, decrease heart rate, regulate blood sugar, utilize cortisol more efficiently and lead to effective stress relief. When you face difficulties and expect the best outcome, to not worry or fret over something you cannot control, genuinely believe it will be resolved with good effort, and to not care what others think, then your chances of success are greatly increased.

> *"Nothing is permanent in this world, not even your troubles."*
> CHARLES CHAPLIN

Dr. Judith T. Moskowitz at Northwestern University Feinberg School of Medicine in Chicago found that new patients with HIV infection, who used the Eight Skills to Achieve Positive Outlook, as listed below, showed a lower virus load, better compliance with medication and were less likely to need antidepressants to cope with the illness.

1. Recognize positive event each day
2. Log in journal, savor or tell someone about it (verbalize)
3. Daily gratitude journal/ be thankful/ appreciate
4. List personal strength & how you used it
5. Set attainable goal, sense of purpose & note progress
6. Report on a minor stress & how to reappraise the event positively
7. Recognize & practice small acts of kindness every day
8. Practice mindfulness, focus on present and future, not on the past.

To these, I hope she doesn't mind if I add three more skills:

1. Look forward to doing something nice, to being somewhere pleasant
2. Walk briskly with arms swinging and with rhythm, with pep in your step, whistle, sing, exert yourself, and forget the stressor
3. Smile, lift your spirit, act like you are having a good time and mean it -> changes brain chemistry and stimulates the release of positive hormones.

You have value you are worth something, no matter what. Psychologically, a positive outlook can enhance the belief in one's own abilities, decrease perceived stress and push a more healthful behavior mechanism. Physiologically, a positive view can lower levels of C reactive protein (CRP), a marker for stress-related inflammation. Negative thoughts can trigger the stress response to release excess cortisol that can lead to accumulation, repetitive release and consequent reduced immunity, inflammation and disease. In a change of thinking from negative to positive, the focus should be on the good. While you are at it, go ahead and avoid negative people with negative thoughts. A conscious effort should be made to suppress or reduce the stress hormone response. When things go wrong, focus on the many things that are going right. "The glass is half full", not half empty. Do the black dot test (or white dot, whichever). Do not focus on the dot but focus on the remaining 99% of the paper. Make a conscious effort to reduce the cortisol release.

> *"No amount of guilt can change the past...and*
> *No amount of anxiety can change the future."*
> ARABIC SAYING

Worry and negativity are common responses to stress. The psychochemical reactions generated will lead to inflammation and high blood pressure and eventually to disease. This response will solve nothing as the stressor will still be present. Use every strategy and technique available to rid the mind of ruinous depressive thoughts. The response may be out of context with the stressor or may be along the right lines or maybe totally inconsistent. Stress remains and continues toward a damaging outcome. Rumination, deep thoughts on the causes and consequences of one's distress, is a more focused form of worry. Both fail to address practical solutions.

> *"Worrying is like being in a rocking chair; it gives you something to do, but doesn't get you anywhere."*
>
> ANONYMOUS

In the presence of chronic stress, the stressor is an obstacle. Your response options are: go over or through it (adaptation mind), change it (alteration body), go around it (avoidance), or let it stop you and worry (negative acceptance) or transcend the situation and interpret it in a way that makes sense and works for you (positive acceptance). Stress responses may vary according to individual differences, depending on genetics, nutritional development, access to education and experiences, environment and personal behavior. No one option is completely effective by itself. There is no one correct answer.

One approach in treating stress is to address the source. For emotional causes, address the mind; for environmental causes, address the body. For both, address the spirit through faith, prayer, belief, trust and forgiveness. Choose and use the one or ones that work for you and for the situation.

Vignette #17: *The stress levels of a struggling father, living in poverty with 5 kids, are very different than those of the well provisioned father dealing with a high paying high demanding job. Though both are under duress, the frequency, intensity and duration are quite different as is the response. Likewise, for the 1.5 billion people living in poverty on day to day basis would probably not want to hear about "attention, compassion and gratitude" to relieve their levels of stress, whether physical and/ or emotional. Personalized "mind-body practices", attention training, refined interpretations, psychotherapy, biofeedback, and skills needed for life situations drawn from philosophers and psychologists are probably inappropriate to the world's poverty stricken people.*

Neuroscience relief techniques do not quite play out in the Hood and simple Gratitude is a bit difficult to acquire when you are struggling for basic survival from one day to the next. So I tried to present stress response strategies that are easy to comprehend and utilize in any setting.

> *"If you stumble and fall, just make it part of the dance."*
> GEORGE BANTON, LYRICS

Faith is that personal belief in the existence of a higher element (God) and spirituality is the universal belief that nature is greater than ourselves. When utilized in this way, both can be powerful healing forces. "My faith in Jesus will get me through" exhibits positive chemical changes in the brain. "God doesn't give one more than he/she can handle" and "Faith can move mountains", are mantras that work. Forgiveness has a strong basis in faith. This art of withholding blame or anger toward someone or something is practiced more by the poor and disadvantaged than by the wealthy. Is this the mechanism by which the wealthy continue to expand the inequality gap and keep getting elected to high office? The ability to cease to feel resentment and forgive one's proven enemies is a great achievement in human mental development. Those who can sincerely and truly forgive, can remove a lot of stress from the situation. To forgive someone who entered your church, killed your family out of hatred and showed no remorse, is the height of successful stress response strategies. A lot can be accomplished by the passive response to God's will. *"In sh' Allah"*. Faith, forgiveness and prayer for deliverance from chronic stress imposed by hardships of status, environment and emotional state, are the chief survival mechanisms of oppressed people. The path to salvation and peace leads through God. With these tools one can shape the world into a place where one is safe and sound and free of stress.

Forgiveness as a stress solution is not necessarily attached to any particular religion or faith. In basic Buddhism, the brain is "good to have memory for facts and figures, but greater to have to forgive wrongs and return to harmony" and "Turn poison into medicine", transforming the negative into the positive showcase the effects of the effort.

Forgiveness is vital to the emotional health and survival of the group; without it, conflict, pain and illness reigns. Forgiveness cleanses the heart, mind and soul. Those who do not forgive are physically, emotionally and spiritually deficient and tend to become immersed in sadness, guilt and self-destruction. Returning the hurt that is received can intoxicate and kill. For some, forgiveness is the most difficult of the strategies in route to a stress-free life. But clearly, when genuine, sincere and complete, it is the most rewarding. When you dismiss the stressor, it is gone and can no longer harm you.

Carrying a grudge and seeking revenge take up a lot of negative energy, cause periodic or constant releases of stress hormones and keep one in a perpetual state of unease. Though these are clearly physiologically unwanted states, they are so much easier to slip into than forgiveness. Throughout history, revenge has been depicted as an effective means of neutralizing a stressor. "Avenge not yourselves...vengeance is mine, I will repay, sayeth the Lord." Romans 12:19. Yet, only God, as the ultimate judge, can take revenge. "Repay no one evil for evil, but give thought to do what is honorable in the sight of all. If possible, so far as it depends on you, live peaceably with all." Romans 12: 17-21. In Homer's *Iliad*, Achilles, mad at Hector for killing his companion, Patroclus, so plots his revenge. "Anger... that for sweeter than trickling honey wells up like smoke in the breasts of men." XVIII.109. "Do not say, 'I will do to him as he has done to me; I will pay the man back for what he has done'". Proverbs: 24:29. For Dame Agatha Christie in *Murder on the Orient Express*" for each one, the plunge of the dagger was sweet."

Revenge and reward are recurrent motives in human affairs. Why do we feel the urge to sing in the streets after the death of a hated person? According to Marcus Aurelius, "The best revenge is to be unlike him who performed the injury." By a slightly different form for Euripides in the tragedy, *Medea* "Hell hath no fury like a woman scorned" and in *The Mourning Bride* by William Congreves (1697), "Heaven has no rage like love to hatred turned nor hell a fury like a woman scorned". These show promises of the intensity of the revenge that is to come. Shakespeare's productions are loaded with instances of revenge as is all of history.

"Do not resist an evil person. Whosoever strikes you on your right cheek, turn the other to him. For whosoever wants to sue you and take your shirt, give him your coat as well. Love your enemies, do good to those who hate you, bless those who curse you, pray for those who mistreat you," Matthew 5:39, takes us back to forgiveness. Not only is the act physically and mentally rewarding, but in a functional society, it is the right thing to do.

Yet, our laws imprison criminals for five reasons: 1) punishment for a crime, 2) rehabilitation, 3) as deterrence to others, 4) as protection of the society against more crimes and, 5) as revenge on behalf of the victims. Turning the other cheek is not a part of the picture. When those family members of the Charleston, South Carolina church murderer said "they" forgave him, the society did not. He sits alive in a protected prison cell, comfortably breathing and awaiting the elements of revenge.

Harboring resentment is unhealthy. It releases bad stress hormones that harm the immune system, inhibits proper thinking, affects proper digestion, and results in dysfunctional metabolism. If you offend someone, apologize, get rid of it, and remove it or it will make both of you bitter and sad. If you are offended, forgive. It is not because they deserve it, it's because you do. Forgiveness is not an act to let the person who harmed you off the hook, but to end the grief, anger and pain you are suffering.

> *"Holding a grudge is like taking poison and ex-*
> *pecting the other person to die."*
> BUDDHIST SCRIPTURES

But it is when you have to forgive a person who isn't even in the least bit sorry, that this particular strategy is difficult to effect. What if revenge and forgiveness are used together?

One of the subtlest yet effective examples of revenge for an ultimate wrong lies in Marc Anthony's eulogy on the murder of

Julius Caesar. In his reference to Brutus, "this was the noblest Roman of them all" ...he forgives Brutus, while at the same time, highlighting the depth of his betrayal, and leading ultimately to his untimely demise.

> *"Before you embark on a journey of revenge, dig two graves."*
>
> CONFUCIUS

Nearly all organized religions counsel against revenge and advocate love for one's enemies. In its penchant for continuous wars, human society has all but buried this concept. The hypocrisy is blatant. "Love thine enemies as thyself" and "Forgive those who trespass against us" are spoken by the devout but rarely ever followed. In reality, revenge prevails and chronic stress is its reward.

For those who firmly believe in freedom from religion, when faced with the stressor, they rely more heavily on coping strategies of adaptation and alteration. In the absence of organized religion, the individual may resort to inner spirituality and self-control when formulating the positive over the negative.

Forgiveness has power and purpose in the relief of the stress of guilt and of revenge. However, society's humans appear to have learned to live without it. Forgive the Nazi's, the American slaveholders, the pioneers who massacred the natives on four continents, or the Turks who killed defenseless Armenians. Forgiveness should be easy as a way of healing one's wounds through compassion, patience, knowledge, understanding, empathy and tolerance. Instead many opt for hatred, revenge, intolerance, negativity and evil. What kind of world would we have today is the response to 911 had been one of forgiveness?

Forgiveness heals both the bestower and the receiver. Forgiveness at the Charleston church massacre did nothing to change the receivers in that society. Their guilt, anger and racism are as strong and florid as ever. Forgiveness only works for the bestower who can use total acceptance to "turn the other cheek" as a means of satisfaction, without regrets.

The forgiveness policy of Nelson Mandela, who became president of South Africa after being imprisoned for 27 years for opposing apartheid, was truly monumental. And the ultimate can be found in the crucifixion of Jesus of Nazareth, in forgiving his executors during the process of dying, *"Father, forgive them, for they do not know what they are doing."* Even Jesus did not advocate "forgetting". The story of the crucifixion is paramount in the Christian lexicon and a cornerstone in the collective memory of millions. Forgive, but do not forget. In practical usage, remembering the stressor helps to avoid the same situation in the future and provides physical protection. Secondly, in not forgetting the stressor, and who, what, where and how, one can maintain self-respect and provide emotional protection.

One can also go beyond forgiveness, in praying to save the soul of one's tormentor. A victim who would "normally" be forced to use cruelty as a means for revenge, would come to understand and pity the profound unhappiness that would lead a tormentor to perpetrate such wrongs and offer prayers. To accept everything that is thrown at you, as "God's will", is passive acceptance. Though different from active prayer and search for relief, it works just as well.

Suggested Stress Relief Prayer of the Day: "Great Spirit, thank you for making me strong through adversity. I thank you that because you are faithful to me, I can be faithful to you. Give me your wisdom to make the right decisions today, and the strength to stand strong, no matter what life brings. Amen."

Volunteering to pray for others in expending energy to help others is rewarding to both parties and is stress relieving. In Quantum healing through long distance prayer, management of energy fields, mind-body communications and paranormal phenomena, the effects on stress relief are being investigated. Although faith, forgiveness, and prayer limit the effect of stress on tissues and organs, in most cases the stressor is still present.

Gratitude is the art of giving thanks and the state of appreciation. In practice, one cannot feel stress and gratitude at the same time. If gratitude can outpace stress as a response it can be utilized as an effective solution. Taking time to express gratitude for your life and breath, for daily living, to appreciate nature, and to be thankful for God's work, works in the long term to relief stress.

> *"Taking time to contemplate exactly what you are grateful for isn't merely the right thing to do. It also improves your mood because it reduces your cortisol output by 23%"*
> TRAVIS BRADBURY

ADAPTING TO CHALLENGE WITHOUT BREAKING: Purpose, Meaning, Plan, Organization, Journaling, Daily mantra, Behavior change, Grounding, Reframing, Relaxation, Nature Walks, Meditation, Quality Sleep, Hobbies, Gardening, Guided imagery, Volunteering, Music, Aromatherapy, Color and Expressive Art therapy

THE MIND

Adaptation is a stress management strategy in which the mind changes the response from negative to positive by engaging in some task or practice that increases internal energy levels, providing they are already present. A wandering, idling brain without consolidated memories of organized thoughts will remain out of focus and ineffectual. A healthy network that lights up in the presence of direct thinking and formulation of a plan toward a purpose will quicker attain results than one that is unhappy. An unhealthy person is unable to focus on the goal of controlling or eliminating the stressor. A brain that worries about the past and agonizes about the future is incapable of planning, problem solving or handling overwhelming stress. The goal-oriented brain that puts aside sadness, guilt, anxiety and regret, has a much better chance of changing negative thoughts into positive ones and to monitor the external world (from within) for safety against potential threats. *To deal with stress effectively, "I'll never get through this" must be replaced with "this too shall pass".* In developing a stress-free attitude, face it intelligently and practically prepare for it. There should be no *"I didn't see it coming"* reaction.

There are many how-to manuals for dealing with stress adaptation techniques. The Harvard Medical magazine, the Mayo Clinic book and numerous online sites all offer courses, pamphlets and therapy sessions on coping with anxiety, depression and stress, which are very effective, assuming they "fit" your status, environment and condition. Mostly they address the response and are light on the stressor. Prevention is hardly mentioned. Most stressors and stress responses do not fit neatly into this scenario. Access to a guided imagery or a cognitive behavior therapist in some communities may not be a viable option.

One must first recognize the stressor, the source and the probability of success. Then decide on a stress response strategy or strategies and gain confidence in your good health. The stronger you are in body and mind, the more efficient the response. Start with a mantra or a group of mantras. Something simple like "I deserve better!" and "this is my situation and not my final destination!" will work to stimulate the mind to go further. "All situations are temporary, I can survive anything temporary" and "there is no wrong decision, only consequences" will accompany deeper thinking.

Buying a house, choosing a mate, moving to a new location, or choosing a career, all require planning and organization. When faced with a formidable stressor, make a PLAN. Have a purpose, a reason for living, a goal, be it general security, comfort, or happiness. Having specific success at a particular skill may help to identify the problem, decide on the options, set time limits, examine your motives, evaluate the situation and choose your strategies.

ORGANIZE your plans and your time to help you stick to your plans. Face anxieties, put them aside, separate worries from concerns, distinguish minor issues from major ones. Be active, keep your mind busy and involved with the plan directed toward control or elimination of the stressor. Get the facts, tackle the problem, and focus on the present, one at a time. In addition, have a future plan that looks past this stressful situation and forward to something good, like a trip, a pleasant visit, something creative. Take time to pursue personal activities that make you happy and more at ease with yourself. Set small goals which could accumulate to offset the stressful issue. Address the response, face and release emotions. Cry, scream or laugh to remove the stressful chemicals through emotional clearing. Consider engaging in a support group or another person with the experience and willingness to provide assistance and advice. Some stress is due to poor time management. Therefore, schedule what matters most, like time with family and friends, time off, time to relax, time to exercise, time for creativity and productivity. If affordable, buy time to free up some for yourself.

For example, pay others to do the chores, tasks, work you do not wish to do. Buying time is better than buying stuff.

Another helpful tool is JOURNALING. Make two lists: (1) stressors that are draining you and how to deal with each one, and (2) things you enjoy doing to counteract the stressors. Manage your time. Make "to-do" lists. Do not leave loose ends. Complete all tasks. Make and stick to a budget. Feel good about accomplishments. Look forward to completing all. Write down thoughts, feelings, inspirations and aspirations. Use your mind to focus on what is important. Keep a Stress Diary. Stop small problems from growing bigger. Write down threats and physically, symbolically, discard these pages. Write down what is bothering you, stress causing people and events, and how you intend to approach them. Write out a personal narrative of purpose and goals. Read about how others approach similar situations and their solutions. Get negative feelings out of your mind and body. Write at the same time every day and look forward to solving the situation.

> *"I used to hope you'd bring me flowers. Now I plant my own."*
>
> RACHEL WOLCHIN

The Mayo Clinic Guide for Stress free living and other manuals promote "attention training, refining interpretations, cognitive restructuring, anger management, systemic desensitization, electroconvulsive and interpersonal therapy". Some of these techniques may be a bit too complicated for many individuals, especially when bombarded with chronic stress. So in the effort to keep it simple, try Behavioral Change and Life Style Modification. If things are not going your way, change your situation change your response.

First and foremost in change of behavior, is to establish your self-esteem. You are capable. Success is just a question of when, where and how. Second change is to stop using worry as a response to anything. Change the way you think. Direct your energy and thoughts toward problem solving. Examine all parts of the stressor, find its weaknesses, the parts you can deal with and the parts that require other avenues.

Use the strategy of REFRAMING to change the way you look at the situation. In some cancer cases, successful suppression of cell growth rates have occurred when the subject takes on the cancer as his or her own possession, addresses the situation and strives to control it. Finding some good in a bad situation and being assertive toward it really works. By controlling emotional stress, you can influence and reduce cancer outcomes. How you frame the matter has a greater impact than the matter itself. Your response to the stressor greatly influences the outcome. The stress mindset in using coping strategies to build on and learn from experience in a constructive manner will always find more success than the throw up the hands, throw in the towel, and let the stressor control destructive manner. Developing new brain cells for defense, alertness and memory is better than putting the brain in neutral and allowing chronic repetitive damage to tissues and organs.

Reframe and reappraise the situation to make it an opportunity for growth, learning and change. Pay off a surprise IRS debt and do not omit or neglect it again. Overspending on the credit card, pay it off and cancel until you can "handle" it again. A bad marriage, learn the signs and don't do it again.

Some older individuals may use humor to reframe their experiences and maintain their sense of integrity and wisdom in face of the ageing process. They may find success in combining despair and depression with joy and happiness to "reframe" the situation into a life, finding beauty in an ugly world scenario. Be aware that sometimes what may work on the surface, may not work on the inside. It may tear up and destroy the psyche entirely. The great Robin Williams seemingly had so much going for him, in terms of talent, success, and influence. Yet his internal stress mechanisms robbed him of his will to live. So be sincere, genuine and very careful in the use of reframing as a strategy for stress control.

> *"No matter what happens, walk as if you are kissing the earth with your feet".*
> ANONYMOUS

Stay GROUNDED. Things can't be all that bad. Stay connected with reality. When stressed and anxious or depressed, look around you and find 5 things you can see, 4 things you can touch, 3 things you can hear, 2 things you can smell and 1 thing you can taste. Relate with others and share your experiences your good fortunes your connection with reality. In dealing with Stress sometimes it is good to put the burden down, rest a while and plan to pick it up tomorrow, if necessary, *"Sleep on it."*

RELAXATION is one of the best strategies of mind and body adapting to the situation and reducing the cortisol response. Good SLEEP quality and quantity, is the best source of brain rejuvenation and memory management. Sleep ensures the healing and repair of damaged blood vessels and heart muscle, blood sugar regulation, repair of kidney tissue, regulation of circulation and blood pressure to avoid stroke, and repair of brain cells. New memories are created, sorted and stored during sleep. Adequate quantity for the average person should be between 7 to 9 hours. The quality is judged as being able to overcome fatigue and bring about that rested refreshed feeling upon awakening. Restful sleep is influenced by the number of awakenings during the sleep cycle, breathing oxygen intake and relaxation of body frame. Good quality sleep can boost one's mood, improve memory, and reduce inflammation. Sleep can boost creativity and restore especially the emotional components of memory. Physiologically, sleep lowers cortisol and cholesterol level, reduces chronic stress and dangerous high blood pressure, regulates heart rhythms and improves heart disease. On the contrary, less than 6 hours sleep in a cycle can see an increase in inflammation proteins, sleep apnea deprivation of oxygen, and outright insomnia. Sleep is a crucial element of cell rejuvenation and repair. During sleep, the brain removes toxins, maintains nerve connection pathways, files new memories into storage, and fine tunes concentration and responses.

A HOBBY is a very effective form of channeling energy in the right direction, away from negativity. Do something that brings relaxation benefits and that you enjoy. Fun can be its own reward. It can range from building motorized airplanes and cars to playing dominoes, chess or cards with friends; from going all out for golf, to trying new makeup, having a regular manicure or pedicure, fixing your hair, and dressing up or down. Gardening is physical exercise that carries the extra clout of having a mental connection with the plants. Knitting and crocheting entail delicate movements with the distraction and diversion of energy into creativity probably accounting for the stress relief. Stamp and coin collecting and building model planes and boats keep the mind and body occupied and active. Though these activities are proven to limit the damaging effects on tissues and organs, the stressor is still there.

Playing music, reading, painting, and playing board games can bring happiness. Teach and learn. Give or take classes. Remove the "money" factor and just do it for the joy of it.

Reframe and provide your work society with some leisure time specifically designed to reduce stress levels. Attaching real value to the hobby in itself will provide relief.

Take NATURE trips alone or with family and friends. Visit parks. The very essence of nature reduces the stress response. Adequate exposure to sunshine can't do your Vitamin D levels and health any harm. You need it. In terms of quantity, add more relaxation and less work time. Unplug devices for fullest effect.

MEDITATION is the mode of relaxation that focuses on the present and tunes out the stressor. By relaxing both the body and the mind, one can boost the immune system and hasten stress recovery. Cortisol markers measured for traumatic stress disorder (PTSD), anxiety and depression, were found to be significantly lowered after proper meditation sessions. Pain, anxiety and depression were also reduced but with less effects on heart rate and blood pressure. The level of effect depends on the level of meditation attained.

Relatively new attention has been turned to the length of DNA "telomeres" as a marker for longevity. Meditation has significant positive effects on reducing the acceleration of telomere shortening associated with oxidative stress. It can be a major tool in the treatment of anxiety, in reducing the agitation, tension, headaches, and insomnia. Meditation increases alpha brain waves to enable clearer thinking. In a tranquil state, oxygen consumption is reduced and can be replenished. Lactic acid builds up in the muscles is decreased allowing rest and repair. Nerve conductivity is lowered which reduces anxiety and there is a restoration of essential brain chemicals. Brain derived neurotropic factor (BDNF), a natural protein that regulates elasticity of neurons and promotes brain cell development, is abnormally low in those suffering from Alzheimer's, depression and anxiety. Meditation can raise the levels of these proteins.

Once the individual is aware of, recognizes and acknowledges the presence of chronic stress, determines to eliminate the bad feelings and consciously engages the stressor, a time and place for constructive meditation should be chosen. The setting should be a safe place that is quiet and pleasant. The time could be early morning when one is rested or early afternoon to wind down from the day. Your intention should be one of willingness to engage and achieve calm. Sit comfortably with good posture, eyes closed; focus your mind on energy centers in your body and on breathing. Expel bad thoughts from your brain with each exhalation. It helps to expel bad feelings and reduce stress hormones, while secreting and releasing good hormones. Focus attention on present events and on the inner workings of your body and mind. Concentrate on one thing, or one event, a light, a candle or a mantra that is bright and uplifting. Concentration and repetition brings the mind and body together to reduce an abnormal stress response. Your mind needs exercise and rest. You may enjoy tackling a high intensity mind exercise better than just rest. Counting, doing multiplication tables, adding complex numbers can engage the rational brain to block out negative noise and achieve silence. Focus on mental and physical processes intended to achieve relaxation. Solving crossword puzzles is another high brain activity leading to relaxation. When tired of these mindful activities, plan to rest, sleep of function at a lower level of activity.

Discontinue activities and avoid things that prevent or interfere with relaxation. For example, reducing intake of caffeine, saturated fats, excess alcohol, sugar, exposure to fearful sounds, bad news, anxiety-promoting people, horrible sights, stressful events, bad smells and bad meals that contribute to poor digestion, greatly improves the effects of relaxation.

Meditation and mindfulness can attain higher levels of relaxation as in the stages of Buddhism enlightenment. Consider practical means of breathing awareness, body scan assessment, compassion and caring as means of reducing the stress of conflicts on the job, family and financial difficulties, chronic pain and illness, sleep disorders, anxiety, chronic fatigue, and depression.

MUSIC produces relaxation as a general effect through a combination of nostalgia and nerve-soothing sound. It is especially effective for inducing sleep. Stress hormones (cortisol), as measured by salivary and alpha-amylase levels, are reduced and dopamine is increased. Cognitive functions like focused attention, learning and working memory, improve. Music activates specific relaxation centers of the brain, while heart rate, pulse and blood pressure are reduced, and in type 2 diabetics, blood sugar levels are lowered. The spinal cord reacts to sound, both pleasant and noxious. Medium level musical frequencies as with classical adagios and new age music, produce energy vibrations that are potentially linked to health in promoting healing and well-being, and restoring healthy sleep patterns. Listening to music helps to relieve pain. Before research studies were made on its effectiveness, I provided appropriate music before, during and after my surgeries. It worked in reducing patient anxiety and bringing on relaxation. Playing music appears to connect the right and left brain and not only brings satisfaction to the artist, but personal relaxation as well. Music reduces the impact of migraine headaches, helps children with epilepsy, reduces tinnitus, and improves ADD. By improving concentration it is appropriate for reducing stress in repetitive activities (putting the same screw onto the same gasket 200 times an hour). Music has been shown to help with the stress of post-partum anxiety.

GUIDED IMAGERY is a subjective relaxation technique that uses a controlled visualization of detailed mental images designed to reduce the stress response directly in thinking of places and things you enjoy. Imagine yourself in this setting that makes you feel good, calm, relaxed and happy. For me it could be on a cruise shipped with my wife, dressed up for dancing, on a field trip to ancient ruins on a French countryside with vineyards and orchards and herbal medicine plants or on a sandy beach on a clear day under a tree looking at the surf. This simple imagery can help the brain rejuvenate, create new brain cells, and improve nerve cell communication. The brain remembers delightful memories but also negative ones. The drawbacks of guided imagery are that it is time consuming, may require an expert guide therapist and that not much research has been done on the results.

Vignette #18: *When my parents and my older brother all passed away within three month of each other and from preventable conditions, for which I, being a physician, felt the pangs of responsibility and pain of being unable to stop the processes, for the next four months, I painted 55 canvasses in oil and acrylics. With subjects that ranged from a war-torn landscape to a chiffon butterfly, and not having had any formal training or inherent talent for art, that anyone knows of, surprisingly, some of them were good enough to frame and hang in the living rooms of friends and family. The act of preparing and executing a painting that expresses one's feelings either directly or indirectly, can get you through hard times like grieving and lost opportunities.*

EXPRESSIVE ART THERAPY uses creative juices you may not know you had, for rehabilitation, psychological healing, and counseling in what amounts to effective medicine. Creative activity including painting, dance, writing and drama can help to heal the inner self and especially the perceived damage of image. Many forms and techniques can be used in which the physical and the emotional are merged, resulting in an eventual positive outcome. Of 37 studies reviewed, 81% showed positive reduction in the stress response.

COLOR THERAPY explores the influence of colored lighting and painted walls on human physiology and emotions. Soft colors like blue, green and yellow are associated with relaxation and pleasant memories. Blue lighting has a calming effect, reduces sleepiness by suppression of melatonin secretion and in post stress relaxation studies was found to enhance alertness. But too much blue-violet light can also be damaging to the macular cells in the retina through oxidative stress, and color and detailed (reading) vision are affected adversely. Yellow hues are associated with energy, reds with passion that increase the stress response, green is restorative and white is neutral.

AROMATHERAPY is most often associated with relaxation and calming, reduction of both anxiety and depression. Eucalyptus, marjoram, rose, vetiver, Ylangylang, Roman chamomile, bergamot, sandalwood, rosemary, geranium, clary sage, lemon, cedar wood, and especially lavender have all been verified in evidence based relaxation response studies for their calming effects. The brain reacts to aromas through the olfactory apparatus by slowing down, thereby enabling a reduced anxiety reaction and a reduction in negative emotions. The smell of essential oils brings molecules into contact with the nasal canal, where they dissolve into the mucus lining of olfactory epithelium in roof of nasal cavity, from here they are transported to the olfactory cortex and limbic system of the brain and processed as "aroma" for relaxation or agitation. For example, sesquiterpene chemicals in frankincense and sandalwood activate oxygen in the limbic system to stimulate the pineal and pituitary glands to increase the secretion of antibodies, endorphins and neurotransmitters, which all lead to relaxation of the body and mind.

These coping strategies and adaptation are forms of suppression, muting the reaction or pushing away the thought process that would elicit a fear reaction to chronic release of stress hormones. Though indicated for and effective in events like divorces, care of an ageing parent, and high stress job, they are a form of short term relief similar to the use of drugs, alcohol, tobacco, and high carbohydrate foods which provide transient comfort and immediate pleasure. Most adaptation strategies block or delay the effects of the stressor and require repeated application. Like some drugs, repeated use of same agent may lead to addiction or dependence on use. It does very little to alleviate the effects of long term despair and is at most, temporary.

ALTERING THE STRESS RESPONSE PHYSIOLOGICALLY CHANGES A NEGATIVE INTO A POSITIVE: breathing techniques, exercise, yoga, tai chi, social interactions, laughter, altruism, consensual sex, balanced diet, conventional medications, natural medicines, mental stimulation

THE BODY

Exercise, a healthy balanced diet, social interactions and mental stimulation are all natural stress reducers with positive effects on the body physiology. A direct or indirect modification of the chemical response will reduce the intensity and duration of the stress response effect. When you change from the chronic to the acute mode of stress response, the damaging effects are reduced considerably. As with all stress relieving strategies, a strong functional immune system is required to attain the full effect. These strategies change the chemical and physiological response from sympathetic (fight or flight) to parasympathetic (relax and digest). If bombarded by stressor pathogens, you can feel the involuntary action of your strong immune system as it resists the attack and maintains homeostasis; if surrounded by stressors and you voluntarily engage strategies to "change" the situation physiologically and biochemically to turn away the stressor or avert the response; if you "feel a cold coming on" and the resistance to fend it off is just as strong; if you encounter an insult or a stressful event, and feel the aversion as you use an active strategy to alter the stress response, then you have changed the response from bad hormones (cortisol, epinephrine) to good hormones (endorphins, serotonin). Use your mind to think of what makes you happy and content, and actively replace the negative with the positive outlook. Use your body to replace the chronic release of damaging hormones with recovery mode healing endorphins.

My favorite active strategy when confronted with a formidable stressor, such as instigators of road rage, family argument, direct insult or unexpected bill, is to use a controlled BREATHING TECHNIQUE 4, 7, 8. For example, to address the response, clear your head, put the tip of your tongue to the roof of your mouth just behind the front teeth. Breathe in (inhale) through your nose to the count of 4, hold it in to the count of 7, and breathe out (exhale) to the count of 8. Repeat at least four times, then rest. Feel the relaxation and the reduction in cortisol. This is the classic change of sympathetic to parasympathetic response. It works well in traffic, at the office, in the operating room, at home, or anywhere you may encounter a stressful situation. It does wonders for alleviating insomnia and inducing sleep. Other breathing exercises include bellows breathing for acute stress, roll breathing for increasing oxygen levels, and abdominal breathing for chronic stress. Deep progressive muscle relaxation in which muscle groups are tensed and relaxed, one at a time, can bring calm and relaxation to the body as well as to the mind. Controlled breathing boosts the immune system by increasing oxygenation of the blood and tissues, boosts alertness and reduces the levels of stress hormones by inhibiting cortisol release. The yogi's pranayama breathing control promotes concentration and improves vitality. It can be used to treat anxiety, insomnia posttraumatic stress disorder and attention deficit disorder (ADD).

If you can't eat or play with it, just lift your leg, pee on
it and walk away. The Dog's Strategy for Stress Relief

EXERCISE; use the stress response to make you stronger. Change it to benefit your health and make you stronger. Do structured exercise to improve health and get into better shape to handle the release of stress hormones. Take control. Change from whining and weeping and negativity to challenging the stressor, and responding with strength instead of weakness. Increase your energy levels to deal with this one and be ready for the next. Improve your muscles and nerves. Get more oxygen to brain for thinking, problem solving and improve circulation for physical strength. The body and brain release endorphins to burn off excess adrenalin/norepinephrine from vigorous exercise (with sweating), like a good run, basketball or a tennis game and eliminates toxins through perspiration. A good morning exercise will burn off fat calories and the afternoon activity will keep it off, with both getting cortisol levels back to physiologic regulation. In general, aerobics are directed to toned muscles, balance, and flexibility, while weight training converts fat to muscle. Exercise can re-channel the stress response from mental worry into physical well-being. It has a direct positive effect on the immune system in producing efficient white blood cells that respond appropriately to injury and prevent excess inflammation, as well as increasing stress resistance by developing a tolerance and improving the ability of mind and body to handle it. In a research study, mice that exercised for 2 weeks were resistant to a stressor (bullying episode) and showed faster recovery than mice that were sedentary. Exercise induces a pattern of calm in certain parts of the brain and enhances nerve cell rejuvenation.

Exercise is better for heart disease by increasing blood flow dynamics than for weight loss.

A 15 minute walk reduces blood pressure, increases mood, reduces anxiety and allows clearer thinking to "get it off your chest". A 30 minute walk of one to three miles, from A to B to A, three to four times a week, when done routinely, improves the body and the mind. Without exercise there is a loss of oxygenation and blood flow to the tissues, leading to reduced nutrients and a reduction in nerve and muscle cell health. Muscle turns to fat in the sedentary individual. Consistent regular exercise is better than sporadic heavy weight lifting.

For vigorous exercise, a good run releases endorphins (feel good hormones, a second wind), burns up excess adrenalins, boosts mood (endorphins), increases physical strength and reduces the stress response by reducing cortisol levels. Bicycle riding outdoors is preferable for the fresh air, greenery and variable scenery but for exertion, indoors will work as well. Weight training with low weight repetitions and "sets" of "3-10-1" will build strength and tone muscles, nerves and "sinews". (3 weight sets, 10 repetitions with each and 1 minute rest in between pro-duces more endorphins than fewer repetitions with heavier weights). A grouping of 12 body exercises including squats, lunges, push-ups, and planks will cover the basic needs of the body to get and keep in shape. A treadmill with variable speeds and inclines is excellent. Triple sprints of 20 seconds each with 2 minute rests followed by a 3-5k run, on a regular basis, will the chances of Vitamin D absorption in the skin, stimulate the release of endorphins and contribute to the calming effect.

YOGA, stretching, tai chi and qi gong are "release exercises" that combine both exercise and meditation in addressing both the body and the mind. These can be done with classes or through books or on line charts. Start slow, concentrate, do it regularly and achieve success. Yoga poses and positions can reduce levels of C-reactive protein (CRP), a marker for body inflammation, reduce stress cortisol and increase brain-derived neurotrophic factor (BDNF) levels, a protein that promotes the health of brain cells. Twelve weeks of yoga amounting to 90 minutes of pos-tures, breathing and meditation, for 5 days a week, slowed cel-lular ageing. There was an increase in anti-inflammatory mark-ers after yoga and a reduction in pro-inflammatory markers.

TAI CHI, also known as meditation in motion, is a Chinese mar-tial art of defense that is useful for stress management especial-ly for fibromyalgia consisting of body pain, fatigue, stiffness, memory lapses associated with cognitive impairment, sleep problems and post-traumatic stress disorder (PTSD). Its low impact, slow, focused movements are better-suited for chronic pain than aerobics like walking, resistance and strength exer-cises. Mowing the lawn (manual), scrubbing floors, washing cars, scrubbing the tub, and cleaning the garage are all "power exercises" and count for a lot.

SOCIAL INTERACTIONS are very important to good health and body and mind function. Contentment releases oxytocin, a feel-good stress-relieving hormone. whether in the presence of stress or not, enlisting and maintaining a group (2-3 trusted friends) of like-minded people with similar experiences provides support, diversion, problem-solving help, discussion and coordinated responses often needed in stressful situations. Love, friendship, a strong marriage and family cohesion are an integral part of the support group. When indicated, find an experienced mentor, a role model who can be "trusted", family, clergy or counselor. Express yourself, present your problem and work out a solution based on viable suggestions. Face fears, do not despair and give up. Express anger when you need to, accept advice, find meaning and purpose, attach to it and always move forward. Invariably, the very act of expressing will make you "feel better" after "getting something off your chest. Accept invitations, attend conferences, learn, attend museums, visit new places. Do not be afraid of others. They are just like you. We are all the same; we laugh and cry for the same reasons. Connect with others. Shunning and avoiding others is unhealthy. Be especially attentive to your partner. Hugging and holding hands with the person you love has been proven to reduce stress almost instantly.

Communicate effectively. Listen first, talk less, listen more and then answer. Do not dwell on the past, complain or criticize too much. Most people have a low tolerance for hearing complaints over and over. Find good things to say or say nothing at all. If you have ailments, accept them as a part of life. Do not make pain and discomfort the entire focus of your existence. If you have strong beliefs, savor them, but do not force them on others. Live your faith, do not export it

Be aware of real versus false friends. Make new friends, open relationships, identify strong versus weak friends. Be aware of those who give and those who take. Associate with positive people. Take a lesson from the Greeks. "Philotimo", sharing what you can afford to share, "philoxenia", hospitality as the right thing to do, and "agape", not expecting anything in return for doing something good for others, establish this society as having one of the healthiest outlooks on life and subsequent lowest stress levels.

> *"If you find you are too much for some people to take; those aren't your people."*
>
> ANONYMOUS

Disrespect, rudeness and personal affronts drive up stress. Having adequate support in your life can help you stay healthy and good health is the cornerstone in the defense against stress. Spending quality time with people who make you feel good plays an important social role in reducing stress levels.

> *"It is more blessed to give than to receive".*
>
> JESUS OF NAZARETH, ACTS 20:35

ALTRUISM, being good to others, has its own rewards.

VOLUNTEER. Join in the service of others, give positive thoughts as well as whatever essentials you can afford, to those less fortunate. Your psychological esteem, how you feel about yourself, will increase. Your health, life satisfaction, state of mind, positivity and social standing itself will improve. "Little things help" and "what goes around comes around". The sincere intention of helping others will in turn help you to feel better spiritually, emotionally and mentally.

Treat the stress of LONELINESS by inviting yourself to be with other people, in person or on social media. Get involved by volunteering at a soup kitchen, local market or community groupings. Join art therapy or organized nature walks. Find and hang out with fun people. Live independently but not alone. Engage and socialize with neighbors, family and friends. Join a book club or a walking group. If you have the slightest interest in music or dance, join a group of like-minded people. Being active contributes greatly to reducing the stress response.

> *"A good laugh and a long sleep are the two best cures for anything".*
>
> IRISH PROVERB

LAUGHTER, real and genuine, activates chemical reactions that can alter the stress response through the release of brain chemicals (endorphins). Like a "runners' high", the act of laughing stimulates multiple organs by increasing oxygen intake levels, heart rate stimulation, and lung respiration. Tension is soothed by stimulation of blood circulation and muscle relaxation. Released endorphins act as natural painkillers. An increased neuropeptide release boosts the immune system and reduces cortisol accumulation. Laughter activates the acute stress response which then follows with recovery and a relaxed feeling. A good laugh relieves depression, is a sigh of relief from danger and clears the mind. Laughing can be used in social situations to show others you like them, you understand them and you connect with them. Instead of being negative and pessimistic after a bad experience, use it to learn and choose to laugh at the fact that life can sometimes get the better of us. One laughs some 30 times more frequently, more intensely and tends to be contagious when in a group, than when alone. A baby giggles when tickled at around 3 to 4 months old, well before it speaks. Laughter is an effective communication to friends and strangers alike. Though it may be taken offensively by one's enemies, laughing when under pressure may be an effective strategy. (It makes your enemies wonder what you are up to). Life is wonderful, savor it, be grateful.

When not laughing, wearing a smile is good for the facial muscles and warms the heart. For me, "I am fortunate to have seen my patients turn gray." I try to smile as often as I can, especially in the office. It is a lux to find humor in all situations. Sometimes it takes a bit of maneuvering, but look for it nonetheless. There is immediate gratification in the presence of Puerto Ricans and Greeks who smile at and with you on brief encounters. The verbal offer of a *"Buen Provecho"* over your meal in a public restaurant or at a roadside pause is pleasing and gratifying. The American sourness in an elevator or restaurant conveys fear and loathing and results in the immediate production of stress hormones.

Consensual SEX for the purpose of mutual satisfaction and pleasure will provide the individual with an improved mood (serotonin release), reduced anxiety (reduced cortisol) and relieved body (release of endorphins and sex hormones). Physical intimacy reduces stress better than with an orgasm alone. In situations of high stress, the libido is low, and less sex is associated with more stress. Sex lowers blood pressure levels and there is less of an increase during stressful events. Sex lowers the cortisol release more than in the same situation without the act.

NUTRITION: A well-balanced diet is important in providing the body and mind with the fuel and energy needed to manage the chronic stress response. If the body is healthy enough, many stressors are ineffective in producing damage. A diet high in fresh fruit and vegetables can provide antioxidants to neutralize damaging free radicals. Small multiple meals of lean proteins and whole grains provide energy for optimum metabolism.

Good fats, omega -3 fatty acid foods, Vitamin C and E- rich foods provide the immune system with the ingredients it needs to prevent most diseases. Then there are the comfort foods, like chocolate, macaroni and cheese, ice cream, sugary drinks, cookies, high in glucose, serotonin, dopamine and tryptophan that activate the pleasure centers and reduce stress. However, an overload of sweets can have detrimental effects. Yes, stressed spelled backwards is "desserts".

Table 6. WELL-BALANCED DIET for STRESS RELIEF

Turkey & chicken	Fruit & vegetable	Cold water fish
Berries	Nuts & seeds	Chinese soups
Organic meats	Quinoa	Beans & legumes
Whole grains	Flaxseed	Olive oil and avocados
Egg yolks	Milk	Chocolate

The anthropologist, Bronislaw Malinowski, conducted a study in Papua New Guinea, in 1914. In 23000 subjects on a high fat diet (40-60%), there was no instance of cancer, diabetes, obesity, dementia, or hypertension. He concluded that essential fatty acids (EFA) in the diet increased the immune system to the point that when under duress, the body is able to compensate and maintain equilibrium. Good fats like avocado and coconut oil, contain polyunsaturated oils, alpha linolenic acid, and linoleic acid that promote healthy cell membranes, optimum DNA function for growth and repair of cells, cholesterol metabolism, blood clotting, blood pressure regulation, hormonal balance and thyroid function. They regulate reproductive health, liver and kidney function, nerve, hair and skin health, and contribute to a reduction of mood and behavior disorders.

Table 7. FOODS THAT INDUCE ANXIETY & STRESS

White sugar, flour & rice	Artificial sweeteners
Saturated fats (cream, butter, whole milk	Red meat, pork, lamb (fatty cuts)
Processed meat (salami, sausage,	Alcohol and drugs
Lard	Skin on chicken

Soy may upset ones hormonal balance, especially in women. Coffee beans that are heavily fertilized and treated with pesticides will act as an anxiety promoting nervine stimulant. Decaffeinated brews made with chemicals are not good. Likewise, some liquors are tainted with contaminants and too much will damage the liver and upset the insulin regulation. Sugar competes with Vitamin C for white blood cell regulators and can adversely affect the integrity of the blood. Processed and refined foods contain toxins with potentially detrimental neurological effects. Many of these contain L-canavanine, which stimulates the immune system to produce inflammation in the body.

Table 8. FOODS THAT REDUCE THE STRESS RESPONSE

Oatmeal	Blueberries & bilberries	Turkey & chicken
Avocado	Broccoli & cabbage	Salmon & mackerel
Almonds & walnuts	Oranges, grapefruit, lemon, lime, kiwi, tangerines	Borage and coconut oil

Good stress response foods reduce anxiety hormones, increase calming hormones, reduce blood pressure and increase the function of the immune system. Oatmeal and turkey stimulate the release serotonin, a feel-good hormone, in the brain. Blueberries and bilberries are antioxidants that reduce oxidative stress. Complex carbohydrates like whole grains and pastas and simple sugars like sweets and sodas also release serotonin, but caution in overuse leading to inflammation and obesity is a concern. Avocado is a good fat with high potassium content that helps reduce high blood pressure and anxiety. Broccoli and cabbage are *Brassica* vegetables with high folic acid contents that reduce stress, anxiety, depression and panic. Fatty fish like salmon and mackerel are loaded with omega 3 essential fatty acids that prevent cortisol and adrenaline accumulation. Almonds and pistachios contain healthy fats and B vitamins, magnesium, zinc and Vitamin E that all help with serotonin production and immune system boosting. Citrus fruit are high in Vitamin C which reduces circulating cortisol levels and borage oil inhibits abnormal adrenalin release. Chewing raw vegetables when you can reduces tension in the jaw in addition to added vitamins and minerals.

Table 9. IMMUNE SYSTEM ENHANCERS

Botanicals	Probiotics	Nutrients	Spices
Hygiene	Hydration	Sleep	Laughter
Sunlight	Mindset	Exercise	Music

Astragalus, basil, oregano, garlic, rosemary, ginseng, Echinacea, elderberry, pau d'arco, myrrh, licorice, suma and green tea are botanicals with evidence-based association with boosting the immune system. Probiotics aiding with digestion and absorption are plain yogurt, kefir, kimchi, kumbacha and sauerkraut.

Immune system building nutrients include fruit like papaya, pomegranate and citrus which are high in Vitamins C, A and E; nuts and seeds like almonds, Brazil nuts and cashews high in selenium; vegetables like broccoli, kale and red bell pepper, and proteins like lean beef, skinless poultry, and shellfish.

Spices that reduce the inflammation response include cayenne, turmeric, ginger, cinnamon, black pepper and cloves. Good hygiene keeps the body free of microbial contaminants. Hydration aids in digestion and maintains tissue integrity.

Sleep is essential in minimizing the effects of stress. It raises essential metabolic hormones and reduces cortisol. Laughter increases blood circulation, stimulates digestion, decreases muscle tension, and increases immune T cells and antibody production, while it reduces cortisol levels.

Adequate exposure to sunlight facilitates the absorption of Vitamin D that promotes immunity. Regular exercise 3 times a week, actively increases a positive mindset, releases endorphins, increases blood circulation and reduces oxidative stress. Listening to relaxing music increases the release of immunoglobulin A; antibodies that aid in the immune response.

Table 10. HERBALS and MINERALS for STRESS RELIEF

Calming infusions (lemon balm)	Strong relaxants (skull cap)
Antidepressants (St John's Wort)	Antistress Minerals (magnesium)
Nervines (black cohosh)	Sleep (valerian root)
Aromatherapy (lavender)	Adaptogens (Ashwagandha)

Lemon balm (*Melissa officinalis*) is considered by many to be the best of the calming infusions. Others include catmint, lime blossom, chamomile, and passionflower. Strong relaxants include vervain, with its antispasmodic activity, cowslip, valerian, skull cap, and kava, all with action against anxiety, insomnia and nervousness. St John's Wort is an effective sedative in cases of mild depression and reduces localized inflammation. Wild oats is also a mild antidepressant and has wound healing effects Magnesium is considered to be the "relaxation mineral" and along with calcium, reduces the stress response. In the presence of adequate amounts of B vitamins, zinc, potassium and Coenzyme Q10, a vital nutrient in energy production, stress symptoms are expected to improve. Natural botanical nervines that reduce the activity of overstressed nerves work best for environmental stressors like heat, cold, altitude, humidity and weather-related extremes. Black cohosh, cramp bark, skull cap, and lavender can improve the emotional and physical performance responses to stressors.

An infusion of hops, valerian, passionflower, and lemon balm on a regular basis, can enhance the chances of good quality sleep. Red clover and chamomile tea is good for children. The aromatherapy essential oils, lavender, frankincense, rose, vetiver, ylang-ylang, bergamot and clary sage have relaxing effects that help relieve stress and promote sleep.

Adaptogens is the term invented in the former Soviet Union, for those natural plants which stimulate the body to increase stamina and resist stressors. Their products were used extensively and successfully in their aeronautical space projects. Originating, growing and thriving under stressful environmental conditions, these plants produce phytochemicals that modulate and reduce adverse stress responses.

Table 11. ADAPTOGENS, primary

Ashwagandha (*Withania somnifera)*	Siberian ginseng *(Eleuthero-coccussenti-cosus)*	American ginseng (*Panaxquin-quefolius*)
Rhodiola rosea	*Panax ginseng*	*Schizandrachinensis*
Licorice root *Glycyrrhiza-glabra*	Maral root *Rhaponticum-carthamoides*	*Cordycepssinensis*

Though there are many listings for adaptogens, the above table identifies the ones most studied and evidence-based. In adhering to the definition of an adaptogens both as natural or synthetic; it is a phytochemical substance that facilitates the stabilization of physiological processes and the promotion of homeostasis through decreased cellular sensitivity to stress. It is non-toxic in normal therapeutic doses, reduces inflammation, prevents oxidation caused by free radicals, and produces a non-specific state of resistance in the body to physical, emotional or environmental stress. It works through the same Central Nervous System complexes that produce the stress hormones. Adaptogens are used primarily for stress response reduction in prevention of anxiety and depression; organ and immune system protection; and support of the thyroid, pituitary and adrenal gland function, and work best in cases of physical and mental stress due to environment and workload. These are very complex plants with differing modes of action as some work by relaxation and others by stimulation, in keeping with what stresses the plant is experiencing. Taking adaptogens in the presence of chronic stress increases the body's ability to cope on cellular level with physical & mental stress, but is not a substitute for basic good health through the other basic strategies of nutrition, exercise, social connections, mental stimulation, and avoidance of toxins.

Ashwagandha (*Withania somnifera*), also known as Indian ginseng or winter cherry, comes from the roots of a nightshade plant and reduces the anxiety component in the stress response, as well as fatigue and stress-induced insomnia. It is readily available in tincture and capsules.

Rhodiola rosea with some 140 phytochemicals, including active rosavin, rhodionin, and salidroside, boosts and modulates the immune system, reduces the release of stress hormones, increases the body's resistance to physical, emotional and environmental stressors, counteracts inflammation, reduces fatigue eases anxiety, builds stamina and enhances cognitive function.

Schizandra chinensis berries can be calming and stimulating at the same time. It is used to promote lung and liver health while calming diarrhea and gastrointestinal upset. It enhances athletic performance and muscle recovery through its action on the central nervous system.

Panax ginseng, Chinese ginseng, stimulates and improves cognitive function, strengthens the body, enhances physical performance, reduces mental and physical fatigue, restores vitality, boosts a depleted immune system and is recommended especially for chronic stress.

Eleutherococcus senticocus, Siberian ginseng, improves and prolongs stamina, reduces stress by rejuvenating the adrenal glands, improves sleep quality, enhances immunity against colds, flu and other common infections, and helps move stress hormones toward "normalcy". *Panax quinquefolius*, American ginseng, with similar ingredients (ginsenocides) to its Asian counterpart, is very effective in reducing fatigue especially in people with chronic illness.

Rhaponticum carthamoides, Maral root, is a sub-alpine plant with benefits for memory and learning as well as protection in environmental stress and enhanced recovery in tired muscles. *Cordyceps sinensis* is a mushroom with strong immune system enhancement and anti-stress properties, especially effective on the digestive system. *Glycyrrhiza glabra*, licorice root, reacts to body signaling of excess cortisol by reducing levels produced by the liver and adrenals. It also reduces inflammation in the gastrointestinal tract.

Table 12. ADAPTOGENS, secondary

Uncariator-mentosa (Cat's claw)	*Asphaltum bitumen* (Shijalit)	*Trametes versicolor* (Coriolus)	*Mormordica-charantia* (Bitter melon)
Bryonia alba	*Ganoderma-atrum*	*Magnolia officinalis*	Goji berry
Phellodendro-namurense	*Jasmonium grandiflo-rum*	*Lepidium meyenii* (Maca root)	*Turneradiffusa* (Damiana)
Sea buckthorn	*Gynostemma-penta*	Ginkgo biloba	Muira puima

The primary mechanism of stress reduction activity of adaptogens is through the release of Neuropeptide Y and Heat shock proteins from neuroglial cells, an action which blocks stress hormones (cortisols), reduces the effect of norepinephrines, and normalizes the immune, central nervous and endocrine systems.

The challenge is to measure the amount of stress induced and then measure the reaction, in order to define as "adaptogen" in terms of what degree of action it achieves.

However, when overstressed and unrewarded, as human beings, we find ourselves in a society that tends to cover every deviation from the "normal", with drugs.

Table 13. CONVENTIONAL MEDICATIONS for STRESS-RELATED CONDITIONS

Tranquilizers	Sedatives	Painkillers
Antimalarials	Immune Suppressants	AntiAnxieties
AntiDepressants	Relaxants	Opiates

Before you turn to legal or illegal drugs, remember that after the effects wear off, the cause of stress will still be there. The very nature of stress is repetition and continuation until a disease state or effective management strategy ends the sequence. The adverse side effects of conventional medications of antidepressants, sedatives, relaxants and tranquilizers are too numerous to list here. Sedatives and tranquilizers (like benzodiaprines), are indicated for panic attacks, persistent anxiety unresponsive to non-medicinal therapies and underlying mental illness and should be used accordingly and with caution. Nonsteroidal Anti-inflammatory drugs (NSAIDS like ibuprofen and naproxen) and anti-malarials should only be used for inflammatory conditions like joint pain with fever, and immune suppressants (like methotrexate) should be used in severe conditions. Anti-anxieties like buspirone, anti-depressants the selective serotonin reuptake inhibitors (SSRIs), norepinephrine and dopamine reuptake inhibitors (NDRIs), serotonin norepinephrine reuptake inhibitors (SNRIs), monoamine oxidase inhibitors (MAOIs) and tricyclic depressants work by blocking the production of inhibiting chemicals and allowing more of the reactive chemicals to stay around. Antibiotics like doxycycline can be used to treat the fear and anxiety of PTSD by disrupting the formation of negative thoughts in the brain and so relieve the stress response. The benefit of Valium and Prozac lies in masking the symptoms and getting you to sleep while curing nothing. When you awaken and recover, the stress is still there until the next dose. In addition, the risk of overdose, dependency, chronic use/abuse, interference with metabolism and other essential medications is high. In all cases, one should discuss the use of supplements and medications with your physician.

Western society produces and allows huge amounts of stress within its population, then provides pills to "suppress" or "alter" the reaction, instead of addressing the causes and reducing the frequency and intensity of stressful situations via lifestyle and societal changes.

This book recommends all natural treatments of stress. To prevent and regulate adrenal gland fatigue, blood pressure control is of the utmost importance. Adrenal gland hormones like aldosterone and corticosterone should be regulated, and electrolytes balanced naturally or by physicians if severely unbalanced. Vitamin regimens for stress should include the B vitamin complex, especially Vitamin B5 (panthothenic acid) that deals with stress and provides energy to adrenal glands. In addition, there are natural plant products, the adaptogens Ashwagandha, Cordyceps, Eleuthero root, and licorice that help with adrenal and liver function.

The most abused and dangerous response to stress is that of self-treatment with alcohol, mind-altering drugs and painkillers. People turn to over the counter drugs for stress relief for many reasons, such as when there is no knowledge or awareness of the presence of natural treatments, no trust in or access to doctors, high expense, ignorance of the condition, too busy, ease of purchasing over-the-counter pharmaceutical drugs, and ease of obtaining stronger illegal drugs. Tradition held whiskey and valium as old stand-byes, recently replaced with Prozac, oxycodone and marijuana as the drugs of choice to reduce stress levels and induce relaxation. Ongoing trials using cannabinoids to relieve or reduce the levels of agitation in Alzheimer's, anorexia nervosa, anxiety, dementia, PTSD, are giving positive results, but minimal to negative results for the psychotic symptoms of Huntington's disease, Tourette Syndrome, dystonia, and Parkinson's dyskinesia. There is a positive association of low levels of stress with chronic cannabis use. With salivary cortisol measurements, cannabis acted at the HPA axis system to reduce the cortisol release and reduce the stress response. If you must use something to "take the edge off", try herbal teas and vitamin supplements.

Table 14: ANTI-STRESS
VITAMIN REGIMEN

Vitamin C	Vitamin E
Calcium	Magnesium
Potassium	Zinc
Tryptophan (5 HTP)	Vitamin B1 (thiamine)
Vitamin B12 (cobalamin)	Borage oil

Vitamins C and E are excellent antioxidants, calcium, potassium, zinc and magnesium regulate and improve nerve flow and muscle relaxation dynamics, tryptophan in turkey breast, wheat germ, granola, and oats, helps prevent insomnia and borage oil, an omega 3 essential fatty acid inhibits abnormal adrenalin release. Vitamins B1 and B12 from vegetables, dry fruit, and whole grains target anxiety control, by regulating the flow of electrolytes in and out of nerve and muscle cells, and regulating digestion and carbohydrate metabolism.

With all these supplements and natural remedies, one still needs a lot quantity and quality to get desired effect. When the chemicals wear off, the stressor is still there.

By far the best choice of strategy left to us is AVOIDANCE. Do not get into the situation in the first place.

AVOIDANCE: avoid or remove the stressor

"Qui a deux femmes perd son âme. Qui a deux maisons perd sa raison."

(He who has 2 wives has lost his soul. He who has 2 houses loses his mind). No matter what, there is stress both ways.

If faced with or in the middle of a stressful situation, when possible, move out of harm's way, leave the scene, change your lifestyle and location, and get on with your life. Focus on removing or disabling the stressor. "The best path to a stress-free life is not to encounter any stress along the way." This is the author's preview of where this is going. The best way to handle any stressor is with this response or "pre-sponse", that is, have no stress in the first place.

But then, we have already admitted that stress is an integral part of life and cannot be avoided. However, it can be significantly reduced. First, you can try to avoid the situations that lead to and compound stress and second, you can control how you respond to a stressful situation. In avoidance, you must be aware of the causes and know what strategies are available to you.

Look at your particular stress history, how you responded in the past, and your success or failure rate. First, if response #1 didn't work, don't keep trying it for the same or similar situations.

2nd: Know what usually causes YOUR Stress.

3rd: Make effort to avoid getting into the same situation.

4th: Make changes in your life to avoid the same results.

5th: Identify which coping strategies work and which ones don't.

6th: Simply avoid situations in which all strategies are unsuccessful.

7th: Actively manage the situation. BE AWARE of the stress hormone release mechanism and make a conscious effort not to engage it.

8th: Put a value on "things". If it's not worth it, don't do it.

9th: Avoid confrontation: KMS (keep mouth shut). Be aware of excesses, extreme limitations or difficult accesses. Either way, they usually do not turn out well.

AVOID Bad habits especially in dealing with others.

1. Stop comparing yourself to others as everyone has a different history and different circumstances.

2. Listen to others (active listening)/pay attention, make the effort to understand and thereby Avoid misunderstandings an prejudging. The lives of others are not your experiences.

3. Do not gossip and Avoid accepting gossip from others. Rumor and here-say are usually incorrect, damaging to any and all relationships and intended to hurt. Ignore what others say about you as they are just jealous of your appeal, your accomplishments and will try to bring

you down to their level. Be aware that they have no idea about your true history, your memories, your interactions, your triumphs and defeats. They are merely trying to hurt you to satisfy their own small minds.

4. Do not wander aimlessly; it is sure to bring nothing but trouble. Have a goal, a purpose, and concentrate, be productive and get results.

5. Do not procrastinate, delay or put off a project no matter how small.

6. Avoid people not worth your time or energy. Replace negatives with positives.

"You are not required to set yourself on fire to keep other people warm"

The Swedes for their "Lagrom" and the Danes for their "Hyyge" are lauded and applauded for having perfected these states of harmony, where you bother no one and no one bothers you. They achieve individual contentment without inconveniencing others. The balance of moderation, with attention to the association of health and contentment, is truly remarkable.

Avoidance advice can be derived from some of my personal experiences. Buy that big house but with heavy safeguards, says your inner voice. Avoid it: *Do not buy the house at all, as it is out of your range and taste. Rent it.* Recognize the potential stress before it grabs and swallows you up.

Hire that person and make him/her a partner, no matter what his/her past. You need them now.

Avoid: *He back-stabbed and double-crossed his previous partners and single-handedly destroyed the reputation of the business.* Don't do it. No matter how urgent it may seem. Find someone else with a more secure resume.

Vignette #19: *Anti-stress exercise: You are at a stream of running water, pristine surroundings, nobody knows this secret place, far away from the hectic workplace and bothersome people. The water is so clear; you can easily make out the face of the person whose head you are holding under the water.*

On your approach to Stressors: Rate the stressor, then remove or avoid it. "Do I really need this?" Avoid contact with people with agitated minds, those who are upset and upsetting. They will surely give you stress. Find those who are centered and calm, and hopefully not too boring. Avoid situations that potentially lead to stress, like property ownership, high-strung jobs, with constant demands that seem unreasonable, demands that require pleasing others, that require dealing with others, that require repeated applications, rules and regulations that are constantly changing since they make no sense in the first place, that deal with "egos", competition, rivalries, situations that will more often than not, lead to hatred and jealousy by others. Avoid harsh environments that require stringent repetitive stress responses. Avoid possible financial quagmires where you know there is a possibility of failure and ruin. Say "No" to stressful projects and to taking on potential problems, especially those of somebody else. Delegate tasks, simplify, unclutter, and downsize.

Avoid all situations with potential difficulties that would *"lead you to drink or engage in other activities that would ultimately create stress in your life."*

1. Do not borrow money you know you cannot pay back.
2. Do not lend money you know you will never see again (give it instead).
3. Do not lend money to family and friends and expect it to be paid back.

4. Do not buy more than you need (property, cars, etc).
5. Get rid of things that could potentially cause problems in the future.
6. Do not offer to get involved and solve other peoples' problems.
7. Do not engage with someone (a stressor) you know will cause you stress.
8. Do not get involved in potential stressful situations.
9. Do not put all your finances in one place. Develop diverse sources of income (rentals, real estate, investments with returns, syndications, multilevel business, other passive sources) so that one stressful situation will not ruin you.
10. Do not let your expenses outstrip your income; avoid buying high maintenance stuff, do not acquire what you can't care for.
11. Do not spend more time working than time enjoying (balance is the key).
12. Spend quality time with family and friends.
13. Develop trust in someone to reduce the fear of "others".
14. Pursue hobbies.
15. Give freely and reap the joys of giving back.
16. Avoid the temptation of artificial food and synthetic drugs to deal with stress.
17. Avoid a state of poor health. Sick is stress in which nothing reduces the stress response.
18. Remove or neutralize the stressor. Ignore it. Give it another label and deal with it (faith, spirituality and belief in something higher). Put something better in its place.
19. Avoid useless competition. Work together. Stop hating "others". Realize once and for all that everyone is human and should be granted the same chance and access

and opportunity and needs your cooperation for all to succeed.

20. Avoid risky behavior. Know your limitations, respect yourself. No sky diving over age 60, no marathons, no deep-sea diving, no mountain climbing, no race car driving and no night clubbing with twenty-year olds.
21. Do not take on projects that require far more time and effort than you are able to give.
22. Beware of foolproof investments, especially from family. It's not easy to walk away from this kind of debt.
23. Don't worry about the children of grandchildren -> you gave them nourishment, shelter, education and support, now it's their responsibility to earn their own way.
24. Adjust your lifestyle to handle what may come your way. The choices you make about the way you live will affect your stress level. Your lifestyle itself may not be preventive but will affect how you recover from the stress.
25. Consider a change of venue, a change of direction and purpose, a shift from job to home
26. Avoid laying blame on extraneous situations which you got yourself into as a cause of stress.
27. Seek opportunities to express and experience the things that make you happy.

AVOIDING THE STRESSORS AND STAYING HEALTHY ARE THE BEST WAYS TO AVOID STRESS.

Note seen on a T-shirt, recently: *"No job, no money, no goals, no problems"*. Though it seems cute and humorous, it is not entirely practical. Purpose, productivity and contentment are natural human traits that are necessary for survival.

CHAPTER FIVE
PERSONAL STRESS-FREE LIFE PLAN

"The greatest weapon against stress is our ability to choose one thought over another."

WILLIAM JAMES

A s rational human beings we can make choices. We have the ability and knowledge to choose between several strategies to alleviate the burdens of chronic stress. Perhaps cognitive behavioral therapy or psychology group sessions or behavioral feedback is not for you. When bombarded with multiple treatments, including medications and accompanying side effects, it is best to step back, assess the situation and proceed logically and intelligently with a Plan for Stress Management.

STRESS-FREE LIFE PROTOCOL TEMPLATE

1. STRESS CONTROL:

Boost and maintain a Healthy Immune System
Keep a Positive Outlook
Practice Faith, Forgiveness, Prayer, Gratitude
Organize your time, practice time management,
Create Plans, with Purpose, Meanings, and Goals

Work-life balance, Daily mantras, Do Journaling
Stay in the present & look to a future free of stressors
Reframing, Grounding, Behavior change,
Quality Sleep, Meditation, Relaxation,
Hobbies, Gardening, Park and Nature Walks
Music, Guided Imagery, Visualization
Art therapy, Aromatherapy
Breathing exercises, Mind and Body Workouts,
Social Interactions, Laughter, Consensual Sex.

2. EXERCISE:

Walk for 30 minutes a day, 4 days a week; Practice Yoga, Tai chi, weight training, aerobics, running, rowing, swimming, gardening, vigorous dance

3. NUTRITION:

Balanced Diet, good local food, high in vegetables, fruits and grains,
Weight control, fresh Natural foods as medicines
Vitamin B complex and Vitamin C,
Herbal teas for Inflammation: turmeric and ginger
Relaxation teas: lemon balm and chamomile

4. SOCIAL CONNECTIONS:

Socialize; visit trusted friends, share experiences, share meals, cultivate genuine hospitality, sincere relationships, and altruism.

5. MENTAL STIMULATION:

   Learn new things, Travel, explore
   Exercise your brain, with reading, puzzles, meditation
   Sleep, rejuvenate

6. AVOID EXCESSES:

   Alcohol, smoking, legal and illegal drugs, Toxin exposure
   (environmental air, light and noise pollution, plastics,
   aluminum foils, fertilizers, pesticides in soil and land
   contamination)
   Know your limits: use age related behavior

Do not get into a Stressful Situation in the first place.

Pick and choose all that pertain to you and are within your
scope of understanding, ability and implementation. Do some
or all as you choose and as available, then narrow down to a
basic few reliable strategies. The goal is the relief of stress, to
the point of achieving happiness, good health and satisfactory
well-being.

Stress-free Life Plan Details

For basic **Stress control**:

1. A **positive outlook** is by far the most useful strategy. Be
   grateful for what you have instead of for what you don't
   have. Be glad it is not worse. See the glass as half full,
   not half empty. Organize. Write out a daily plan; check off
   items as done, as you go along. With Journaling, enter your
   thoughts and goals for the day, week, month and year. Do
   it at the same time every day. Always have something to

"Look forward to". Make sure to separate "worries" from "concerns". They are different. Concerns release less stress hormones. Avoid agitators who are upset and upsetting. Have a Purpose. Set goals, explore and establish a meaning for your life. Include happiness, relaxation, and a stress-free existence. Spirituality, faith and religion are helpful here. Learn and practice Meditation with or without guided imagery and other techniques to concentrate on being centered and relaxed. Use Breathing exercise: 4-7,8 formula: Breathe in with mouth open for count of 4, hold it X 7, exhale X 8...do it at least 4 times, then relax. DO this basic exercise every time you feel "rushed", upset, angry or depressed. It works. Use advanced relaxation techniques like abdominal breathing, deep breathing, and progressive muscle relaxation after you master the basic. For Aromatherapy, lavender, clary sage and eucalyptus are excellent relaxers. Basic Stress management works best without conventional or illegal Drugs!!! If you must "take something", use only Natural Herbs or Food supplements.

2. **Exercise**: Set your goal for effective weight control, toned muscles, balance and flexibility with regular physical movement like walking, jogging, biking and workouts. Set a target weight, reach it and keep it. Walk 3 to 5 miles from point A to B to A, at least 4 times a week. In weight training, convert fat to muscle 15 minutes a day with 5 to 10-pound weights. Do basic upper body repetition drills (10 times, rest one minute, repeat 8 times, rest one minute, repeat 8 times, for 4 days a week. Do Yoga exercises in the early morning or evening, 10- to 15 minutes. Do Yoga levels 1 & 2, after you master these, go to levels 3 & 4. Disciplines like Tai chi and Pilates may require some structured instruction. Regularity is essential.

3. **Nutrition**: Eat a local, organic, *balanced* diet with protein, carbohydrates, good fats; lots of fruits, vegetables and grains; drink water before, with and between meals; herbal teas; NO sodas, No fast foods. Small multiple meals (4 to 5) a day, should be directed to building your health especially your immune system with antioxidants at each sitting. Set a target for weight, reach it and stay there. The recommended foods for Stress control: oatmeal, blueberries, turkey, almonds and whole grains; avocados, broccoli, salmon, oranges (citrus) and foods with folic acid, B vitamins, C & E and calcium-magnesium citrate. The best Herbals for Stress control: Ashwagandha, Siberian ginseng (Eleuthero root), and Rhodiolarosea at least one daily, usually in capsule form but natural is better. Lemon balm, chamomile, catmint, valerian, St John's Wort, Cordyceps mushrooms, passionflower, and borage oil all have calming effects. Ginger and/ or turmeric tea for inflammation prevention and control, in the morning then; one cup coffee for the day, followed by chamomile-valerian-lemon balm tea at night for sleep.

4. **Social Connections**: Find and keep quality friends you can absolutely trust. Stay in touch via email if you must. Use Sunday mass or weekly sessions to increase bonding with like-minded people. Volunteer for a charity. Share meals. Laugh…either by yourself or with someone else. Share a hobby. Travel with a group. Regular is better than sporadic.

5. **Mental Stimulation and relaxation**: Reading in quality time is an excellent exercise for your brain. Resume or attain an interest in history, biographies, and how-to hobbies that challenge your intellect, such as collecting, making and investigating. Travel! Explore new places and meet different people. If confined or otherwise limited, travel in your

mind. Visit a virtual country every day on your computer and keep track of your favorites. Absorb everything. Assign a purpose and meaning to everything you encounter. Learn a new language. Learn to play a musical instrument. Good quality Sleep is the most important activity for brain rejuvenation and arrangement of memories. Use relaxation teas, lemon balm, chamomile, passionflower, and valerian on a regular basis, they have other health enhancing qualities as well. Reduce loud sounds. Dine earlier. Sleep foods like turkey breast, wheat germ, granola and oats activate relaxation hormones. Leave at least 2 hours for digestion, then sleep. Aromatherapy with a diffuser with lavender, vetiver, chamomile, ylang-ylang, cedar wood, sandalwood, is good for relaxation. Use indoor plants that remove toxins like formaldehyde, benzene and toluene in our plastics and fabrics. Snake plant/ tiger's tongue (*Sansevieratrifasciata*), Rhododendrons, Peace lily *(Spathiphyllum)*, and spider plant (*Chlorophytumcomosum*) are some of the best.

6. **Avoidances**:

Say No to stressful projects.
Say No to stressful people.
Do not borrow what you can't pay back.
Do not lend what you need.
Do not take or put yourself in any situation that will compromise your health.

> *"Happiness shouldn't be a goal, it should be a habit"*.
> RICHARD BRANSON

(All is well and good and easy to say when you have a couple of billion dollars lying around and nobody to annoy you)

A stress-free life offers relief, not necessarily happiness. Achieving happiness is a difficult matter to figure out. To be truly happy is to find one's place in life where one feels comfortable and in harmony with the environment as well as with who we are. Most importantly, it is knowing how to be satisfied and grateful for some semblance of peace in this life. Nirvana, enlightenment and Heaven can be attained in the next.

> *"Ultimate goal in this life is happiness without cost."*
>
> ANONYMOUS

There are worldwide differences in attitude, approach and reaction to a Stressor. Everyone lauds and applauds the Swedes for their "Lagrom" and the Danes for their "Hygge". They have perfected these states of harmony where you bother no one and no one bothers you. The balance of moderation aimed at enjoyment, with attention to health and contentment at same time. They achieve individual contentment without inconveniencing others. Perhaps the harsh environment triggered and empowered this harmonic state and enabled such an achievement.

In Japan, close knit families, friends, organized groups, social circles, and a strong community sense of belonging provide a security that greatly reduces stress levels. In Singapore, China and Korea there are "therapeutic parks" where rest and relaxation and group tai chi reduce stress and increase mental well-being. In Spain, the mid-day "siesta" not only helps with digestion, but also provides physical and mental rejuvenation in preparation for the evening exercise, dining and socializing. In Switzerland there is a strong sense of well-being and collective pride in good health. Factors used in the UN Happiness Report of 2016, in which Denmark won, GDP per capita, social support, healthy life expectancy, freedom to make life choices, generosity, and trust. The latter was the most important factor that separated countries and individuals in the "measurement "of happiness. The perception of "others" as a threat was highlighted as an impediment to a stress-free life. Spending time doing things that are important, purpose and meaning was a close second followed by a sense of community, socialization and belonging. Countries that placed importance on acquisition of materials, money, winning so that someone else could lose, and exclusion, were at the lower end of the list of achieving happiness.

A completely Stress-free Life may not be realistic, but several communities have come close. Ikaria in the Greek Dodecanese islands, Sardinia, Okinawa, Japan, Costa Rica and Loma Linda, California, are some of Dan Buettner's "Blue Zones", where people live well into their 100's and enjoy relatively stress-free lives. These are areas in the world that contain the highest number of centenarians, who usually conform to healthy habits forming a lifestyle of permanent behavior with effective results. These are the six basic strategies that include regular exercise, local basic organic nutrition free of toxic food, social support that allows each to be a part of the whole, effective stress avoidance or management, mental stimulation and low exposure to toxins. The results are communities largely free of heart disease, cancer, dementia, obesity, arthritis and diabetes. On my recent visit to Ikaria, I was struck throughout by the relative absence of stress as a major factor in the expression of the good health of the populace. Though diet, exercise, social connections, mental stimulation and an environment relatively free of toxins are important, it was the stress control that allowed and drove the impetus to quality health and subsequent longevity.

What does it feel like, this stress-free life?

> *"It feels like a nice quiet pew at the back of an empty church."*
>
> PHILIP KERR

Making your own "Blue Zone" beginning with your personal stress-free protocol will depend on the situation, emphasize some strategies over others, and be determined by your personality, motivation, location and immediate environment. Use these thoughts and strategies to construct your own personal Stress-free Plan, with your own "potential", the stress-free life that is appropriate for you and that YOU can attain realistically.

> *"The greatest weapon against stress is our ability to choose one thought over another."*
>
> WILLIAM JAMES

To set up a personal stress-free life plan, use the template to circle of check off the strategies you will be using. Identify your personal Stressor(s) and the root causes. Track your stressors to see what your historical responses have been, what coping strategies you used in the past, and which ones were successes or failures. Make two columns, a (+) and a (-). Fill in the strategy and shift until the positives outweigh the negatives. Think about WHY you need and want to reduce stress, what it is doing to your health, to your relationships, to your security, comfort and happiness. Choose the stress responses best suited to you, the place and situation that makes you most content, and concentrate on using these strategies on a regular basis: Stress Control,

Exercise, Nutrition, Social Interactions, Mental Stimulation and Toxin Avoidance.

My Personal Stress-free Life Plan: using all six basic strategies

1. Stress Control: Identify the stressor. Maintain positive outlook, with purpose and meaning. Get rid of negative thoughts or change them. Organize and practice time management. Do Journaling, Set up a specific organization of daily life, write at same time every day, to include my thoughts and goals for the day or the week or month; separate "worries from "concerns" and replace worry with concern; count on and plan for setbacks (Plan B & C); Use "avoid and alter" strategies to remove the stressor; focus on what calms me, like farming, gardening, preparing and enjoying meals, your partner, socializing, travel, culture, writing, creativity, reading, knowledge, discussion. Stay healthy. Get good quality sleep, rest, nap, relax, 6-8 hours daily for brain and body rejuvenation; Stay in the present and look to a future free of stress. Do nature walks, music, expressive art, aromatherapy (lavender and peppermint), breathing techniques, laughter and consensual sex as needed.

2. Exercise daily. Two to three hours in the mornings on the farm climbing, digging, weeding, sowing, harvesting, and cleaning. Afternoons, 15 to 30 minutes with yoga, tai chi, weights, exercise bike (while reading). Keep moving.

3. Balanced Mediterranean style diet of local, organic vegetables and fruit, careful and enjoyable preparation of recipes with turmeric, garlic and olive oil with at least one meal; daily herbal teas; include at least one superfood* daily; one cup of organic coffee between 7 and 9 in the morning to offset the cortisol response, provide antioxidants and prevent

cancer. Allow at least 2 hours for digestion after dining. Eat lighter and earlier. Occasional use of adaptogens.

4. Socialize with family, friends and like-minded persons; keep in touch; do bother to keep close. If unable to do so in person, use social networks. Get support, expression, approval, and encouragement for projects. Start and keep discussions going. Spend time with cheerful people. Give advice, not criticism. Plan travel and visits. Avoid being alone, isolated, confined to company of one group only (segregation). Diversify, include, reach out and communicate with others. Always have something good planned.

5. Mental stimulation with daily reading (science and social studies in the morning, mysteries and novels in the evening). Study and create medical and allegorical situational stories. Acquire knowledge and share. Travel, explore new places and meet new people; if confined, then travel in your mind using a virtual computer, keep track of your favorites; learn a new language, musical instrument or new hobby. Exercise your brain through puzzles, games and quizzes. Know enough to be involved in discussions.

6. Avoid areas with known air pollution (cigarette smoke and vehicular emissions), toxic artificial food, areas that use fertilizers and pesticides; know your limits in acting according to age and ability; stay in my comfort zone. Avoid negativity. Avoid agitators who are upset or upsetting. Do not lend money if possible give it when necessary. Do not spend what you don't have. Do not behave beyond your age.

See Superfoods in your Kitchen in Appendix 3

Use positive feedback to congratulate yourself when successful. Applaud avoidance successes. You can actually change the biochemistry of the stress response with positivity. Be grateful for what you have instead of for what you don't have. Be glad the situation is not worse. Stay clear of conventional and illegals drugs. Use only natural herbals or good quality food supplements.

Goals of a Stress-free Life are to:

Sleep easy and awaken in a room with a view
Eat healthy and enjoy it, preferably with others
Spend time doing what makes you happy, and
Every day is Sunday
Smile, laugh, sing and dance whenever you wish to
Complete your bucket list without regret or trepidation
Balance peace and quiet with reasonable exploration and
adventure
Enjoy your partner for mutual benefit, emphasize
good memories, keep love going, love life,
Pride that is not in excess or injurious to others,
is healthy and not a sin
Make new friends, keep old ones close
Keep neat and clean, up to date, physically fit and trim
(well maintained)
Set up and use your stress free life plan daily

Last word; Stay well. Keep a Healthy Life. Without one's health, all else is immaterial. Do the six basic strategies of good health: exercise, nutrition, social interactions, mental stimulation, stress control and avoidance of risky behavior. It is the body, mind and spirit together that make up total health and well-being. This advice is consistent with advice given over the centuries concerning the Human Condition, and how to survive in a society of humans. Ones DNA is programmed for survival at all costs, even if it means inflicting stress upon their neighbors and receiving it in return. Your own personal stress-free plan may offer some measure of protection against these assaults.

> *"A true stress-free life is not knowing what day it is, and not caring."*
>
> ANONYMOUS

SUMMARY

Introduction

Stress is a state of mental and physical tension associated with physically and emotionally challenging events. It is the stress response that determines the effects upon the organism.

The biochemistry of the Central Nervous System's (CNS) release of chemicals in reaction to a stressor, the physiological response of the mind and body of the organism, determine the pathological effects.

The causes of stress are a part of daily life and are extensions of environmental and emotional states.

The stress response is relative to recovery or disease and may lead to successful relief or failure. Its management can be approached on the basis of the six strategies of healthy living: exercise, diet, mental stimulation, social connections, avoidance of risky behavior/exposure to toxins, and choice of stress control.

Statistics reveal that the *USA is a failure in all 6 strategies*, due to sedentary lifestyle, bad food/poor quality diets, low education pursuit, low knowledge base, electronic lifestyle, poor social interactions as based on a high degree of hatred, fear, tribal behavior, bias, and bigotry, high stress levels, and high exposure to toxins leading to high inflammation levels contributing to disease conditions. It is noted that some countries/communities excel in social connectivity, some in physical activities and others in basic nutrition, contributing to longer life spans.

Personal Stress-free Life Plan: positive outlook and organization. Alteration and avoidance are the best solutions for management of Stressor & Response for the individual or group.

Chapter One: Biochemistry & Physiology of Stress

Stress involves a cause (usually external) and a response (usually internal) consisting of the release of specific hormones through the Hypothalamus-Pituitary- Adrenal system with feedback to recover, if acute and to continue releasing if chronic.

Cortisol is the primary stress hormone.

Physical and emotional stress responses are biochemical in origin and elicit physiological effects.

Oxidative Stress occurs at the cellular level and is a major contributor to accelerated ageing.

Environment & Genetics play major roles in stress.

Chronic Stress can lead to Inflammation and serious illnesses.

Stress levels can be measured and logged in as evidence-based science.

Chapter Two: Causes of Stress

Stressors may be Environmental or Social, Physical or Emotional, Acute or chronic

The frequency, duration and intensity may vary depending on where you live/ how you live/and the character of the environmental and emotional influences.

Typical causes include: personal relationships, job, financial, Status in Society, fear of threat, poverty, wealth, inequality (real & perceived) type of cause may determine type of response or cause exists as part of life or as part of society.

Chapter Three: Stress & Disease

Direct link -> tissue inflammation leads to disease/infections, organ dysfunctions

Indirect link -> tissue inflammation associated with organ weakness -> susceptibility to disease

Immune System weakness and malfunction increases susceptibility to disease

Acute response: good inflammation necessary for resolution -> (+) recovery or demise

Chronic response: link to recovery and link to each disease link development (Cancer, Cardiovascular disease, Diabetes, Arthritis, degenerative neurological diseases, autoimmune diseases (Lupus), Dementias, GI tract are Oxidative Stress diseases (slow or no recovery) due to dysfunctional absorption of nutrients which lead to further organ complications.

The body and mind may respond differently to the same stressor.

A major goal of stress management is to boost immune system function and prevent or reduce chronic inflammation.

Chapter Four: Stress Management

The ability to respond and type of response depends on the physiological make-up of the individual and his or her ability to choose an appropriate response.

The success of the response depends on a variety of factors.

The type of stressor, the health status of body and mind (immune system), the availability of strategies, the mindset, social network and support and the environment (risky behavior, exposure to toxins) are key factors in determining the outcome.

The ultimate goal is relief and return to a state of harmony.

Using Acceptance of the stressor, as in ignorance is bliss, or a passive response as in it is God's will, as well as forgiveness is very effective when it is genuine and sincere.

Adaptation of the response to suit the stressor works well but is short-lived and of little benefit for the resolution of the effects of chronic stress.

Rechanneling behavior, reframing, using social support, problem solving together, organizing a strict regimen that has purpose and meaning, separating worries from concerns; all help to alleviate the intensity of the response.

With Alteration, the stressor is accepted but the response is actively changed.

Exercising the body and the mind, implementing a positive outlook, staying on a healthy nutritious diet, using breathing techniques, yoga, strategies of laughing, music and art therapy, all help to change the biochemistry of the body and mind from a sympathetic to a parasympathetic response, thereby reducing stress hormone levels, increasing the immune system to a functional level and eliminating toxins that would contribute to adverse chronic stress.

Faith and prayer actually change the biochemical make-up of the stressor and the response from bad to good, and influence the immune system response as well. Together they are very powerful tools for the relief of physical and emotional stress in all societies.

The use of conventional medicines (pharmaceuticals), are optional and not recommended due to their temporary action and high incidence of adverse effects. Natural and herbal medicines are much preferred but their effects are also temporary.

Avoidance is by far the most effective strategy in stress management. Avoid the situation in the first place. Downsize, re-organize, eliminate, say No to stressful projects, delegate unpleasant tasks, avoid bad food, bad habits, risky behavior, inappropriate age-related activities.

Strive for achieving and maintaining homeostasis, harmony, peace, relaxation and stress-free creativity.

Chapter Five: Personal Stress-free Life Plan

A Personal Stress-free Life plan is presented and provided in the form of a chart, on which the reader can choose and check off the strategies best suited to his/her lifestyle and purpose.

Good Health is a strong deterrent to a poor stress response

A review of my personal choices for a stress-free life is given in more detail with explanations of each strategy impacts everyday life choices and experiences.

The Stress-free Life Plan Protocol, based on the Six Basic Strategies for Good Health, is again presented for copying and posting on bulletin board or fridge for daily reference.

STRESS-FREE LIFE PLAN

1. STRESS CONTROL:

Maintain a Healthy Immune System,
Keep a Positive Outlook
Practice Faith, Forgiveness, Prayer, Gratitude,
Organize your time, practice time management,
Create Plans, with Purpose, Meanings, and Goals
Work-life balance, Daily mantras, Do Journaling
Stay in the present & look to a future free of stressors
Reframing, Grounding, Behavior change,

Quality Sleep, Meditation, Relaxation,
Hobbies, Gardening, Park and Nature Walks
Music, Guided Imagery, Visualization
Art therapy, Aromatherapy
Breathing Exercises, Workouts, Yoga, Tai chi,
Social Interactions, Laughter, Consensual Sex.

2. EXERCISE:

Walk 30 minutes a day, 4 days a week; Practice Yoga; Tai chi;
Weight training, aerobics, running, rowing, swimming, gardening, and vigorous dance.

3. NUTRITION:

Balanced Diet, good local food, high in vegetables, fruit and grains
Weight control, fresh Natural foods as medicines; Vitamin B complex and Vitamin C, Herbal teas for Inflammation: turmeric and ginger, Relaxation teas: lemon balm and chamomile.

4. SOCIAL CONNECTIONS:

Socialize, visit trusted friends, share experiences, share meals, cultivate genuine hospitality, sincere relationships, altruism.

5. MENTAL STIMULATION:

Learn new things, Travel, explore; Exercise the brain; reading, puzzles, meditation; Sleep, rejuvenate.

6. AVOID EXCESSES:

> Alcohol, smoking, legal and illegal drugs, Toxin exposure (Environmental air, light and noise pollution, plastics, aluminum foils, fertilizers, pesticides in soil and land contamination; know your limits: use age related behavior.

Do not get into a Stressful Situation in the first place.

PHYSIOLOGY OF THE STRESS RESPONSE

Autonomic Nervous System:	Sympathetic action
Pupils dilate	Brain releases cortisol
Saliva decreases	Dry mouth
Respiratory passages widen	Pancreatic insulin reduced
Heart accelerates	Voluntary muscles contract
Digestion inhibited	Bone marrow produces more white blood cells
Liver releases sugar to blood stream	Spleen releases more red blood cells
Kidney releases adrenalin and noradrenalin	higher blood pressure
Bladder relaxes	more fatty acids in blood
Rectum contracts	

APPENDIX 2
COMMON EFFECTS OF STRESS ON YOUR HEALTH

1. High Blood Pressure: rise in blood pressure from the release of excess stress hormones (cortisol, epinephrine, adrenaline, norepinephrine), blood vessel constriction and increased heart rate
2. Heart: cardiovascular strain, usually job related/ high demand low decision making
3. Brain :atrophy of brain tissue in areas that regulate emotions & self-control
4. Headaches: tension, migraine/ vascular changes
5. Stroke :high risk / vascular narrowing of arteries
6. Seizures: triggered by stress-related sudden drop in BP (paradox)
7. Memory (decreased ability to form new memories/ cortisol interferes with neurotransmitters responsible for communications between brain cells
8. Insomnia: sleep disorders, difficulty getting to sleep and staying asleep
9. Cravings: increased food intake
10. Digestion: Irritable Bowel Syndrome, constipation +/or diarrhea
11. Fat storage, weight gain, obesity: increase size of fat cells and deep abdominal fat

12. Blood sugar increases, high fasting blood sugar levels (FBS) and blood sugar spikes
13. Hair: graying, thinning, pulling out
14. Pregnancy: increased incidence of premature labor
15. Skin: acne outbreaks, psoriasis, associated with stress-related androgens as triggers
16. Back pain: epinephrine increases muscle tension, ready to fight or flight, anger & mental stress
17. Premature aging: stress associated with shortening of telomeres (caps at ends of chromosomes) and resultant increased cell aging
18. Colds: virus- stressed immune cells are less sensitive to hormones that turn off inflammation, therefore inflammation continues
19. Asthma: stress amplifies immune response to triggers like pollen, dander, and dust
20. Job performance: negative effect on productivity and satisfaction
21. Sex drive decreased, sex appeal decreased attraction to one who is stressed out

APPENDIX 3
SUPER FOODS IN YOUR KITCHEN

Food	Uses
1. Turmeric & Ginger	Anti-inflammation
2. Moringa	(All 20 amino acids, vitamins, minerals, anticancer, anti-inflammation)
3. Blueberries	(Antioxidants (flavonoids, polyphenols, carotenoids), Vitamin C
4. Guava	Antioxidants, fiber, lycopene (anticancer), Vitamin C
5. Kale, broccoli, spinach	Vitamin K (bone), indoles (anticancer), antioxidants
6. Salmon, sardines, tuna	Omega 3, Vitamin A, D, selenium
7. Apples	Fiber pectin, boron (bones), "red delicious", high antioxidants,
8. Coconut oil	MCT saturated fat = good energy, lauric acid (antiviral, antibacterial)

9.	Green tea	Catechins (anticancer), anti-oxidant, relaxant, lowers cholesterol
10.	Flaxseed	Plant Omega 3, lignans (anticancer)
11.	Mushrooms	Shiitake, Maitake, button: have beta-glucans (immunity)
12.	Chocolate	70% dark; antioxidants, magnesium, potassium
13.	Garlic	Allicin (sulfur, boosts production of WBC's immunity, antibiotic, antiviral
14.	Red meat	Protein, iron, selenium, zinc
15.	Sweet potatoes	Beta-carotene, Vitamin C
16.	Beans	Soy, lima, kidney, red, black; protein, Vit B6, Vit E
17.	Roquefort cheese	French paradox: aged, ripened, antioxidant-rich, extends longevity, anti-inflammatory. French women = longest lives in Europe
18.	Oats, cereals	Whole grains, fiber, Vitamin B complex, iron, minerals
19.	Yogurt	Plain, non-fat, calcium, probiotics for digestion, (add berries)
20.	Eggs	Sulfur, protein
21.	Mixed nuts	Walnuts, almonds, flaxseed, omega 3
22.	Citrus	Oranges, mandarins, grapefruit, Vitamin C

BOTANICALS FOR STRESS

American Ginseng	Elderberry (acute)
Citrus, Vitamin C,	Turkey tail
Echinacea (acute)	Omega- *3*
Goldenseal	Kelp
Turmeric	Garlic
Ginger	Cinnamon
Dandelion	Yucca
Green tea	Hydrangea
Pomegranate root	Eyebright
Grapeseed	Pau d'arco
Devil's Claw	Cat's claw
Mushrooms (Reischi, Maitake, Shiitake)	Astragalus
Rosemary *	Probiotics *(yogurt)*
Licorice	

Recommended Immune System Enhancement Supplements for General Health

Astragalus 470 mg
Vitamin C 500mg
Turmeric 720 mg
Ginger 540 mg
Plus a multivitamin

APPENDIX 5
STRESS-FREE LIFE PROTOCOL TEMPLATE

TITLE	METHOD
1. STRESS CONTROL:	Maintain a Healthy Immune System
	Keep a Positive Outlook
	Practice Faith, Forgiveness, Prayer, Gratitude
	Organize your time, practice time management,
	Create Plans, with Purpose, Meanings, and Goals
	Work-life balance, Daily mantras, Do Journaling
	Stay in the present & look to a future free of stressors
	Reframing, Grounding, Behavior change,
	Quality Sleep, Meditation, Relaxation,
	Hobbies, Gardening, Park and Nature Walks
	Music, Guided imagery, Visualization
	Art therapy, Aromatherapy

	Breathing exercises, Mind and Body workouts
	Yoga, Tai Chi,
	Social Interactions, Laughter, Consensual Sex
2. EXERCISE:	Walk 30 minutes a day, 4 days a week;
	Practice Yoga, Tai chi; weight training, aerobics, running, rowing, swimming; gardening, vigorous dance
3. NUTRITION:	Balanced Diet, good local food, high in vegetables, fruit and grains
	Weight control, fresh Natural foods as medicines
	Vitamin B complex and Vitamin C,
	Herbal teas for Inflammation: turmeric & ginger
	Relaxation teas: lemon balm & chamomile.
4. SOCIAL CONNECTIONS:	Socialize, visit trusted friends, share experiences, share meals, cultivate genuine hospitality, sincere relationships, altruism.
5. MENTAL STIMULATION:	Learn new things, Travel, explore
	Exercise the brain: with reading, puzzles, meditation;
	Sleep, rejuvenate.

| 6. AVOID EXCESSES: | Alcohol, smoking, legal & illegal drugs; Toxin exposure (environmental air, light and noise pollution, plastics, aluminum foils, fertilizers, pesticides in soil and land contamination). Know your limits use age related behavior. |

Do Not get into a Stressful Situation in the first place.

REFERENCES

Agarwal, A., Virk, G., Ong, C. & du Plessis, S. S (2014). Effect of Oxidative Stress on Male Reproduction. *World Journal of Men's Health, 32*(1), 1-17.doi: 10.5534/wjmh.2014.32.1.1

Agyemang, P. & Powel- Wiley, T. M. (2013). Obesity and Black Women: special considerations related to genesis and therapeutic approaches. *Current Cardiovascular Reports, 7*(5), 378–386. doi: 10.1007/s12170-013-0328-7

American Psychological Association. (2015). *Statistics on Stress in America: Paying with our Health.* Washington, DC: Author. The Stress in America Survey, August 2014. (PDF version of document).

Andersen, B. L., Kiecolt-Glaser, J. K., & Glaser, R. (1994).A Biobehavioral Model of Cancer Stress and Disease Course. *The American Psychologist*, 49(5), 389-404.

Anduze, A. L. (2016). *Natural Health & Disease Prevention.* Tulsa, OK: Yorkshire Publishing.

Annameier, S. K., Kelly, N. R., Courville, A. B., Tanofsky-Kraff, M., Yanovski, J. A. & Shomaker, L. B. (2018).Mindfulness and laboratory eating behavior in adolescent girls at risk for type 2 diabetes. *Appetite*, *1*(25), 48-56. doi: 10.1016/j.appet.2018.01.030

Arring, N. M., Millstine, D., Marks, L. A. & Nail, L. M. (2018). Ginseng as a Treatment for Fatigue: A Systematic Review. *Journal of Alternative and Complementary Medicine.* doi: 10.1089/acm.2017.0361

Asea, A., Kaur, P., Panossian, A. &Wikman, K. G. (2103). Evaluation of molecular Chaperons Hsp72 and Neuropeptide Y as characteristic markers of adapto genic activity of plant extracts. *Phytomedicine, 20*(14), 1323-9.doi: 10.1016/j. phymed.2013.07.001

Ash, H., Smith, T. E., Knight, S. &, Buchanan-Smith, H. M. (2017).Measuring physiological stress in common marmoset (Callithrix jacchus).Validations of a salivary cortisol collection and assay technique. *Physiology& Behavior,185*, 14-22.

Baluchnejadmojarad, T., Kiasalari, Z., Afshin-Majd, S., Ghasemi, Z. &Roghani, M. (2017). S-allyl cysteine (of garlic) ameliorates cognitive deficits in streptozotocin-diabetic rats via suppression of oxidative stress, inflammation and acetylcholinesterase. *European Journal of Pharmacology, 794*, 69-76. doi: 10.1016/j.ejphar.2016.11.033

Bellin, M. H., Newsome, A., Lewis-Land, C., Kub, J., Mudd, S.S., Margolis, R. &Butz, A.M. (2018). Improving the care of inner-city children with poorly controlled asthma: What mothers want you to know. *Journal of Pediatric Health Care*, pii, S0891-5245(17)30567-9.doi: 10.1016/j. pedhc.2017.12.009.

Berk, L. S. & Tan, S. A. (2006). Anticipation of complementary positive humor lifestyle behaviors decreases detrimental stress hormones and increases beta-endorphin prior to the actual experience. *FASEB Journal, 20*, 4.Retrieved from https://www.fasebj.org/ doi/abs/10.1096/fasebj.20.4.A382-b [Online Publication].

Bonilla, E. (2010). [Mind-Body connection, parapsychological phenomena and spiritual healing.][Article in Spanish] *Investigación Clinica, 51*(2), 209-38.

Boutain, D. M. (2001). Discourses of worry, stress, and high blood pressure in rural south Louisiana. *Journal of Nursing Scholarship, 33*(3), 225-230.

Brody, J. E. (2017, March 27). A Positive Outlook May Be Good for Your Health. In *The New York Times.* Available from https://www.nytimes.com/2017/03/27/well/live/positive-thinking-may-improve-health-and-extend-life.html

Buettner, D. (2008). *Blue Zones.* Washington, DC: National Geographic Society.

Cacioppo J. T., Fowler, J. H. & Christakis, N. A. (2002). Alone in the Crowd: The Structure and Spread of Loneliness in a large social network. *Journal of Personality and Social Psychology, 97*(6), 977–991. doi: 10.1037/a0016076

Carley, A. (2012). Can journaling provide support for NICU families? *Journal for specialists in pediatric nursing (JSPN), 17*(3), 254-257.doi: 10.1111/j.1744-6155.2012.00336.x

Carol, E. E., Spencer, R. L. & Mittal, V. A. (2017). The relationship between cannabis use and cortisol levels in youth at ultra-high-risk for psychosis. *Psychoneuroendocrinology, 83*, 58-64. doi: 10.1016/j.psyneuen.2017.04.017

Chan, M. (2013*). Be free of Anxiety & Stress: Living a stress-free life.* Bonafide Media.

Childs, E., Lutz, J. A., & de Wit, H. (2017). Dose-related effects of Delta-9-THC on emotional responses to acute psychological stress. *Drug Alcohol Depend, 177*, 136-144. doi: 10.1016/j.drugalcdep.2017.03.030

Cicero, A.F.G., Derosa, G., Brillante, R., Bernardi, R., Nascetti, S.&Gaddi, A. (2004).

Effects of siberian ginseng (eleutherococcussenticosus maxim.) on elderly quality of life: A Randomized Clinical Trial. *Archives of Gerontology and Geriatrics, 9*, 69–73.

Cohen, S., Janicki-Deverts, D., Doyle, W. J., Miller, G. E., Frank, E., Rabin, B. S. & Turner, R. B. (2012). Chronic Stress, glucocorticoid receptor resistance, inflammation, and disease risk. *PNAS,109*(16), 5995-5999. doi: 10.1073/pnas.1118355109

Conklin, Q. A., King, B.G., Zanesco, A. P., Lin, J., Hamidi, A. B., Pokorny, J. J., Álvarez-López, M. J.,...Saron, C. D. (2018). Insight meditation and telomere biology: The effects of intensive retreat and the moderating role of personality. *Brain Behavior Immunity, 70*, 233-245. doi: 10.1016/j.bbi.2018.03.003

Crouch, E., Radcliff, E., Strompolis, M. & Wilson, A. (2018). Examining the association between adverse childhood experiences and smoking-exacerbated illnesses. *Public Health, 157,* 62-68.doi: 10.1016/j.puhe.2018.01.021.

Cuttler, C., Spradlin, A., Nusbaum, A. T., Whitney, P., Hinson, J. M. & McLaughlin, R. J. (2017). Blunted stress reactivity in chronic cannabis users. *Psychopharmacology, 234*(15), 2299-2309. doi: 10.1007/s00213-017-4648-z

Dushkin, M, Khrapova, M., Kovshik, G., Chasovskikh, M., Menshchikova, E., Trufakin, V. Shurlygina, A. &Vereschagin, E. (2014).Effects of rhaponticumcathamoides versus glycyrrhizaglabra and punicagranatum extracts on metabolic syndrome signs in rats.*BMC Complementary and Alternative Medicine, 14*, 33.doi: 10.1186/1472-6882-14-33

Fan, S. T., Nie, S. P., Huang, X. J., Wang, S., Hu, J. L., Xie, J. H., Nie, Q. X. &, Xie, M. Y. (2018). Protective properties of combined fungal polysaccharides from Cordycepssinensis and Ganodermaatrum on colon immune dysfunction. *International Journal of Biological Macromolecules, 114*, 1049-1055.doi: 10.1016/j.ijbiomac.2018.04.004

Feinstein, A. & Dolan, R. (1991). Predictors of post-traumatic stress disorder following physical trauma: An examination of the stressor criterion. *Psychological Medicine, 21*(1), 85-91. doi: 10.1017/S0033291700014689

Ferin, M. (1999). Stress and the Reproductive Cycle. *The Journal of Clinical Endocrinology & Metabolism, 84*(6), 1768–1774.doi: 10.1210/jcem.84.6.5367

Figueroa-Otero, I. (2016).*Spirituality 103, the Forgiveness Code: Finding the Light in Our Shadows.* Bloomington, IN: Balboa Press.

Floyd, K. & Riforgiate, S. (2008). Affectionate communication received from spouses predicts stress hormone levels in healthy adults. *Communication Monographs, 75*, 351-368. doi:10.1080/03637750802512371

Frank, L. L. (2015). Thiamin in Clinical Practice. *JPEN, 39*(5), 503-520. doi: 10.1177/0148607114565245

Franklin, R. A., Butler, M. P. & Bentley, J. A. (2018). The physical postures of yoga practices may protect against depressive symptoms, even as life stressors increase: a moderation analysis. *Psychology, Health & Medicine*, 1-10. doi: 10.1080/13548506.2017.1420206

Gao, X., Cao, Q., Cheng, Y., Zhao, D., Wang, Z., Yang, H., Yang, Y. (2018). Chronic stress promotes colitis by disturbing the gut microbiota and triggering immune system response. *Proceedings of the National Academy of Sciences of the United States of America (PNAS).115*(13), E2960-E2969. doi: 10.1073/pnas.1720696115.

Gaskell, K, (2012). *Dark Side of America* [Kindle Edition]. Retrieved from Amazon.com

Giacobbi, P. R., Stewart, J., Chaffee, K., Jaeschke, A. M., Stabler, M. & Kelley, G. A. (2017).A Scoping review of health outcomes examined in randomized controlled trials using guided imagery *Progress in Preventive Medicine, 2*(7), e0010.doi: 10.1097/pp9.0000000000000010

Glynn, L. M., Christenfeld, N. & Gerin, W. (2007).Recreating cardiovascular responses with rumination: The effects of a delay between harassment and its recall. *International Journal of Psychophysiology, 66*(2), 135-140. doi:10.1016/j. ijpsycho.2007.03.018

Goldstein, D. S. & McEwen, B. (2002). Allostasis, Homeostasis, and the Nature of Stress. *The International Journal of the Biology of Stress, 5*(1), 55-58.

Gremigni, Paola. (2013). Is humor the best medicine? *Humor and Health Promotion.* 149-171.

Groesbeck, G., Bach, D., Stapleton, P., Blickheuser, K., Church, D., & Sims, R. (2018). The Interrelated Physiological and Psychological Effects of EcoMeditation. *Journal of Evidence-Based Integrative Medicine, 23*, 2515690X18759626.doi: 10.1177/2515690X18759626

Guo, J., Yang, C.X., Yang, J. J., & Yao, Y. (2016). Glycyrrhizic acid ameliorates cognitive impairment in a rat model of vascular dementia associated with oxidative damage and inhibition of voltage-gated sodium channels. *CNS & Neurological Disorders Drug Targets, 15*(8), 1001-1008.

Hassett, A. L., & .Clauw, D. J. (2010). The role of stress in rheumatic diseases. *Arthritis Research & Therapy, 12*(3), 123.doi: 10.1186/ar3024

Healthwise, Inc. (1995-2018). *Web MD.* available from https://www.webmd.com/

Hernandez, S., Cruz, M. L., Seguinot, I. I., Torres-Reveron, A. & Appleyar, C. B. (2017). Impact of Psychological Stress on Pain Perception in an Animal Model of Endometriosis *.Reproductive Sciences, 24*(10), 1371–1381. doi: 10.1177/1933719116687655

Herz, R, (2009). Aromatherapy facts and fictions: A Scientific analysis of olfactory effects on mood, physiology and behavior. *The International Journal of Neuroscience, 119*(2), 263-290. doi: 10.1080/00207450802333953

Ho, S. S. M., Kwong, A. N. L., Wan, K. W. S., Ho, R. M. L. & Chow, K. M. (2017). Experiences of aromatherapy massage among adult female cancer patients: A qualitative study. *Journal of Clinical Nursing, (23-24),*4519-4526. doi: 10.1111/jocn.13784

Horiuchi, S., Tsuda, A., Aoki, S., Yoneda, K., &Sawaguchi, Y. (2018).Coping as a mediator of the relationship between stress mindset and psychological stress response: a pilot study. *Psychology Research and Behavior Management, 11*, 47–54. doi: 10.2147/PRBM.S150400

Huynh, M., Gupta, R. & Koo, J. Y. (2013). Emotional Stress as a Trigger for Inflammatory Skin Disorders. *Seminars in Cutaneous Medicine and Surgery, 32*(2), 68-72.

Ishaque, S., Shamseer, L., Bukutu, C. & Vohra, S. 2015. Rhodiolarosea for physical and mental fatigue: a systematic review. *BMC Complementary Alternative Medicine, 12*, 70.doi: 10.1186/1472-6882-12-70

Jayatunge, R. M. & Pokorski, M. (2018). Post-traumatic stress disorder: a review of therapeutic role of meditation interventions. *Advances in Experimental Medicine and Biology.* doi: 10.1007/55842018167

Kondo, M. C., Jacoby, S. F. & South, E. C. (2018). Does spending time outdoors reduce stress? A review of real-time stress response to outdoor environments. *Health& Place, 51*, 136-150.doi: 10.1016/j.healthplace.2018.03.001

Law, M. M., Broadbent, E. A. & Sollers, J. J. (2018).A comparison of the cardiovascular effects of simulated and spontaneous laughter .*Complimentary therapies in medicine, 37,* 103-109.doi: 10.1016/j.ctim.2018.02.005

Lee, M. K., Jung, C. S., Yoon, J. H. & Lee, N. (2018). Effects of resistance exercise on antioxidant enzyme activities and apoptosis-related protein expression of hippocampus in OLETF rats. *Technology and Health Care.* doi: 10.3233/THC-181183

Lee, S. U. (2018). Humor as Wisdom for Reframing Life. *Journal of Religion and Health, 57*(2), 551-560.doi: 10.1007/s10943-017-0535-5

Levy, B. R., Slade, M. D., Kunkel, S. R. & Kasl, S. V. (2002). Effects of positive view of aging on health outcomes and longevity. *Journal of Personality and Social Psychology, 83*(2), 261–270. doi: 10.1037//0022-3514.83.2.261

Lim, K., See, Y. M. & Lee, J. (2017). A Systematic Review of the Effectiveness of Medical Cannabis for Psychiatric movement and Neurodegenerative Disorders. *Clinical Psychopharmacology NeuroScience, 15*(4), 301-312. doi: 10.9758/cpn.2017.15.4.301

Lindblad, C., Langius-Eklöf, A., Petersson, L. M., Sackey, H., Bottai, M. &Sandelin, K. (2018). Sense of Coherence is a predictor of Survival: A Prospective Study in Women Treated for Breast Cancer. *Psychooncology.* doi: 10.1002/pon.4702

Mallen, C. D., Wynne-Jones, G. & Dunn, K. M. (2011). Sickness certification for mental health problems: an analysis of a general practice consultation database. *Prim Health Care Res Dev., 12*(2), 179-182. doi: 10.1017/S1463423610000472

Marie, M., Bigot, K., Angebault, C., Barrau, C., Gondouin, P., Pagan, D.,...Picaud, S. (2018). Light action spectrum on oxidative stress and mitochondrial damage in A2E loaded retinal pigment epithelium cells. *Cell Death Disease, 9*(3), 287. doi: 10.1038/s41419-018-0331-5

Martin, L., Oepen, R., Bauer, K., Nottensteiner, A., Mergheim, K., Gruber, H. & Koch, S. C. (2018).Creative Arts Interventions for Stress Management and Prevention: A Systematic Review. *Behavioral Sciences, 8*(2), 28.doi: 10.3390/bs8020028

Mayo Clinic Staff. (2016, April 21). *Stress relief from Laughter? It's no Joke*. Retrieved from https://www.mayoclinic.org/healthy-lifestyle/stress-management/in-depth/stress-relief/art-20044456

McCaffrey R, & Liehr, P. (2016 Jun). The Effect of Reflective Garden walking on adults with increased levels of psychological stress. *Journal of Holistic Nursing, 34*(2), 177-84.

Minguillon, J., Lopez-Gordo, M. A., Renedo-Criado, D. A., Sanchez-Carrion, M. J., Pelayo, F.

(2017). Blue lighting accelerates post-stress relaxation: results of a preliminary study. *PLosOne.12*(10).doi: 10.1371/journal.pone.0186399

Miles, L. M., Mills, K., Clarke, R., & Dangour, A. D. (2015). Association with Vitamin B12 status with neurological function in older people: A systematic review. *The British Journal of Nutrition, 114*(4), 503-508. doi: 10.1017/S0007114515002226

Mishra, L. C., Singh, B. B., & Dagenais, S. (2000). Scientific basis for the therapeutic use of Withaniasomnifera (ashwagandha): A review. *Alternative Medicine Review5*(4), 334-46.

Moreno-Villanueva, M., von Scheven, G., Feiveson, A., Bürkle, A., Wu, H. & Goel, N. (2018). The Degree of Radiation-Induced DNA Strand Breaks is altered by Acute Sleep Deprivation and Psychological Stress and is associated with

Cognitive Performance in Humans. *Sleep.* doi: 10.1093/sleep/zsy067

Münzel, T., Sorensen, M., Schmidt, F., Schmidt, E., Steven, S., Kröller-Schön, S. & Daiber A. (2018). The Adverse Effects of Environmental Noise Exposure on Oxidative Stress and Cardiovascular Risk. *Antioxidant Redox Signal, 28*(9), 873-908. doi: 10.1089/ars.2017.7118

Occupational Safety and Health Administration (OSHA). (2017). *Statistics on stress and disease.* Retrieved from https://search.osha.gov

Panossian, A. & Wikman, G, (2010). Evidence-based efficacy of adaptogens in fatigue, and molecular mechanisms related to their stress-protective activity. *Current Clinical Pharmaceuticals, 4*(3), 198-219.

Panossian, A., Wikman, G. & Sarris, J. (2010). Rosenroot (Rhodiolarosea): Traditional use, chemical composition, pharmacology and clinical efficacy. *Phytomedicine, 17*(7), 481-93.doi: 10.1016/j.phymed.2010.02.002

Panossian, A., Wikman, G., & Wagner, H. (1999). Plant adaptogens III. Earlier and more recent aspects and concepts on their mode of action. *Phytomedicine, 6,* (4), 287-300. doi: 10.1016/S0944-7113(99)80023-3

Percy-Laurry, A, Altekruseet, S. F., Hossain, M. B., O'Keefe, A. M., Johnson, N. J. & Kamangar, F. (2018).Association between socioeconomic status and tumor grade among black men with prostate cancer. *Journal of the National Medical Association, 110*(1), 53-57. doi:.10.1016/j.jnma.2017.06.019

Pert, C. B. (1997). *Molecules of Emotion: The Science Behind Mind-Body Medicine.* New York, NY: Scribner.

Peterson, C. T., Bauer, S. M., Chopra, D., Mills, P. J. &Maturi, R. K. (2017). Effects of Shambhavi Mahamudra Kriya. a Multicomponent Breath-Based Yogic proactice (Pranayama)

on perceived Stress and general well-being. *Journal of Evidence-based complimentary & alternative medicine, 4,* 788-797.doi: 10.1177/2156587217730934

Pokharel, S. S., Seshagiri, P. B., & Sukumar, R. (2017). Assessment of season-dependent body condition scores in relation to faecal glucocorticoid metabolites in free-ranging Asian elephants. *Conservation Physiology, 5*(1) cox039.doi: 10.1093/conphys/cox039

Pressman, S. D., Cohen, S., Miller, G. E., Barkin, A., Rabin, B. S. & Treanor, J. J. (2005).Loneliness, social network size, and immune response to influenza vaccination in college freshmen. *Health Psychology, 24*(3), 297-306. doi: 10.1037/0278-6133.24.3.297

Razani, N., Morshed, S., Kohn, M. A., Wells, N. M., Thompson, D., Alqassari, M, … Rutherford, G. W. (2018). Effect of park prescriptions with and without group visits to parks on stress reduction in low-income parents: SHINE randomized trial. *PLoS ONE, 13*(2), e0192921. doi: 10.1371/journal. pone.0192921

Selye, H. (1976). *Stress in Health and Disease.* Burlington, MA: Elsevier Science.

Selye, H. (1976). The stress concept. *Canadian Medical Association Journal, 115*(8), 718.

Selye, H. (1975). *The Stress of Life.* New York, NY: McGraw-Hill Co.

Selye, H. (1950). Stress and the General Adaptation Syndrome. *British Medical Journal, 1*(4667), 1383–1392.

Selye, H. (1936). General Adaptation Syndrome: *Nature 138,* 32.

Senchuk, M. M., Dues, D. J., & Van Raamsdonk, J. M. (2017). Measuring Oxidative Stress in Caenorhabditis elegans: Paraquat and Juglone Sensitivity Assays. *Bio-Protocol, 7*(1), e2086.doi: 10.21769/BioProtoc.2086

Shin, H. S., Ryu, K. H., &Song, Y. A. (2011). [Effects of laughter therapy on postpartum fatigue and stress responses of postpartum women].[Article in Korean].*Journal of Korean Academy of Nursing, 41*(3), 294-301. doi: 10.4040/jkan.2011.41.3.294

Sinha, R. (2008). Chronic Stress, Drug Use, and Vulnerability to Addiction. *Annals of the New York Academy of Sciences, 1141*, 105–130. doi: 10.1196/annals.1441.030

Sood, A. (2013). *The Mayo Clinic Guide to Stress free Living.* Rochester Hills, MI: Eclipse Publishing.

Sun, L., Li, X., Wang, F., Zhang, J., Wang, D., Yuan, L.,… Qi, J. (2017). High□intensity treadmill running impairs cognitive behavior and hippocampal synaptic plasticity of rats via activation of inflammatory response. *Journal of Neuroscience Research, 95*, 1611-1620. doi:10.1002/jnr.23996

Snyder, B. A. (1997). Expressive art therapy techniques: Healing the soul through creativity. *The Journal of Humanistic Counseling, 36*(2), 74-82.

Tähtinen, R. M., Cartwright, R., Tsui, J. F., Aaltonen, R. L., Aoki, Y., Cárdenas, J. L.,…Tikkinen, K. A. O. (2106). Long-term impact of mode of delivery on Stress Urinary Incontinence and Urgency Urinary Incontinence: A Systemic Review and Meta-Analysis. *European Urology, 70*(1),148-158. doi: 10.1016/j.eururo.2016.01.037

Thoma, M. V., La Marca, R., Brönnimann, R., Finkel, L., Ehlert, U. &Nater, U. M. (2013).The effect of music on the human stress response. *PLOSOne.* doi: 10.1371/journal.pone.0070156

Tsai, P.-F., Kitch, S., Chang, J. Y., Andrew James, G., Dubbert, P., Vincent Roca, J., &. Powers, C. H. (2017). Tai Chi for post-traumatic stress disorder and chronic musculoskeletal pain: A pilot study. *Journal of Holistic Nursing, 36*(2), 147-158. doi: 10.1177/0898010117697617

Tumuluri, I., Hegde, S. &Nagendraet, H. R. (2017). Effectiveness of music therapy on focused attention, working memory, and stress in Type 2 diabetes: an exploratory study. *International Journal of Yoga, 10*(3), 167 -170.doi: 10.4103/0973-6131.213471

Tung, J. & Barriero, L. B. (2017).The contribution of admixtures to primate evolution.*Current Opinion in Genetics & Development, 47,* 61-68. doi:10.1016/j.gde.2017.08.010

University of Maryland Medical Center. (2000). Laughter Is Good For Your Heart, According To A New University of Maryland Medical Center Study. *ScienceDaily*. Retrieved from www. sciencedaily.com/releases/2000/11/001116080726.htm

Von Berens, Å.,Koochek, A., Nydahl, M., Fielding, R. A., Gustafsson, T., Kirn, D. R., Cederholm, T. & Södergren, M. (2018). "Feeling more self-confident, cheerful and safe". Experiences from a health promoting intervention in community dwelling older adults - A qualitative study. *The Journal of Nutrition, Health and Aging, 22*(4), 541-548. doi: 10.1007/s12603-017-0981-5

Walker, J. & Pacik, D. (2017).Controlled Rhythmic Yogic breathing as complementary treatment for post-traumatic stress disorder in military veterans: A case series. *Medical acupuncture, 29*(4), 232-238.doi: 10.1089/acu.2017.1215

Wei, M. (2017, Oct. 19). Yoga could slow the harmful effects of stress and inflammation [Harvard Health Blog]. Retrieved from https://www.health.harvard.edu/blog/yoga-could-slow-the-harmful-effects-of-stress-and-inflammation-2017101912588

Weil, A. (2011). *Spontaneous Happiness: A New Path to Emotional Well Being*. New York, NY: Little, Brown & Co.

Wójcik, R., Siwicki, A. K., Skopińska-Rózewska, E., Wasiutyński, A., Sommer, E. & Furmanowa.M. (2009). Effect of Chinese medicinal herb Rhodiolakirilowii extracts on cellular immunity in mice and rats. *Polish Journal of Veterinary Sciences, 12*(3), 399-405.

Yavne, Y., Amital, D., Watad, A., Tiosano, S. &Amital, H. (2018).Seminars in Arthritis and Rheumatism: A systematic review of precipitating physical and psychological traumatic events in the development of fibromyalgia. doi: 10.1016/j. semarthrit.2017.12.011

Zhonghua Lao Dong Wei Shang Zhi Ye Bing ZaZhi . (2017, June 20). *[Relationship between occupational stress, recovery experience, and physiological health of nurses in a municipal grade A tertiary hospital].* *35*(6):425-428. doi: 10.3760/cma.j

ABOUT THE AUTHOR

Alfred Lee Anduze, MD is a native Virgin Islander, born in Christiansted, St Croix, and with family roots in France, Puerto Rico, and Eastern United States. As an American/West Indian, he grew up among the great storytellers and fabricators of a small but widespread multiethnic community and acquired an unquenchable love for reading and original stories. While as a practicing ophthalmologist, producing scientific papers for journals and lectures for the international circuit was a vocation, writing original stories has been his passion. After serving his community as Assistant Commissioner of Health, President of the Ophthalmological Society of the West Indies, Assistant Professor of Ophthalmology at University of Florida, Editorial Board of the Annals of Ophthalmology, and lecturing in 32 countries, he acquired an Andrew Weil Fellowship in Integrative Medicine and a Masters certificate in Herbal Medicine. In 2012, he retired to farm medicinal plants and organic coffee in the mountains of Puerto Rico. Away from the halls of conventional medicine, he strongly advocates that the best way to treat disease is not to get sick in the first place. With a basic interest in biology, botany, biochemistry and physics, he is currently in pursuit of the desire for enlightenment available through books and the natural lure of creative writing which rotates around original stories of life in the Caribbean and medical textbooks designed to explain the intricacies of disease, health and well-being in the 21st century, through natural means. In Search of a

Stress-free Life is a presentation recommending the basic strategies involved in the achievement of good health.

He can be reached at:
Alfred L. Anduze, MD
PO Box 776
Maricao, PR
00606
dranduze@yahoo.com